About this book

This book is a step-by-step guide to understanding programs and improving your BASIC. Not everyone wants to write their own programs, but once you understand how BASIC works, it is easy to adapt or debug other people's programs and from there it is a short step to writing your own.

At the beginning of the book there is a short guide to the main BASIC commands, with lots of examples to show how they work. The next part of the book shows how the commands are used in programs to do quite complicated things, such as creating a database, making patterns on the screen and sorting data.

The programs are written in "standard" BASIC, that is, a version of BASIC which, with minor alterations, will work on most microcomputers. There is a guide to converting the programs to work on your computer on pages 10-11 and the conversions for Sinclair computers, which use slightly non-standard BASIC, are given at the end of the book.

Alongside all the programs there are detailed explanations of how they work and of useful techniques and routines which you could use in your own programs. There are lots of ideas, too, for experimenting with the programs and adapting them to carrying out different tasks.

Introducing BASIC

The programming language BASIC consists of about a hundred words. Each word is an instruction telling the computer to do something. To make the computer carry out a particular task you give it a list of instructions and information to work on called a program. You can use only BASIC words as instructions, and you must follow the rules, called the syntax, of the language, too.

In BASIC each line of instructions has a number. The numbers usually go up in tens so you can add extra lines without renumbering the whole program.

```
10 CLS
20 PRINT "STARSHIP TAKEOFF"
30 LET G=INT(RND(1)*20+1)
40 LET W=INT(RND(1)*40+1)
50 LET R=G*W
60 PRINT "GRAVITY=";G
70 PRINT "PLEASE TYPE IN FORCE"
80 FOR C=1 TO 10
90 INPUT F
100 IF F>R THEN PRINT "TOO HIGH";
110 IF F<R THEN PRIN
120 IF F=R THEN GOTO
130 IF C<>10 THEN PR
140 NEXT C
150 PRINT
160 PRINT "YOU FAILED-"
170 PRINT "THE ALIENS GOT
180 STOP
190 PRINT "GOOD TAKE OF
```


Typing in a program

When you are typing a program into the computer you have to type RETURN (or ENTER, or NEWLINE, it varies on different computers) at the end of each line. This makes the computer store that line in its memory and wait for the next line. When you have typed in all the lines of the program you type RUN. This tells the computer to carry out the instructions.

If you type in an instruction without a line number the computer will carry it out straight away, as soon as you press RETURN (or ENTER or NEWLINE). This is called a direct command. For instance, to tell the computer to display the lines of a program you have given it, you type LIST as a direct command. To clear the screen on most computers you type CLS.

You have to be very careful to type programs in accurately. If you misspell any of the BASIC words, or type wrong letters, numbers or punctuation, the computer will not be able to follow the instructions. A mistake in a program is called a bug. Most bugs are typing mistakes, but sometimes they are errors in the logic of a program and can lead to surprising results.

USBORNE GUIDE TO
BETTER BASIC

Brian Reffin Smith
and Lisa Watts

Illustrated by
Graham Round

Designed by Graham Round
Additional artwork by Martin Newton

Contents

Guide to BASIC

On the next few pages there is a guide to the main BASIC commands and how to use them. If you have a computer you should check the commands in your manual as some of the words and rules vary slightly on different computers.

PRINT ▶

This tells the computer to display something on the screen. Letters or symbols should be in quotation marks, but numbers need not be, as shown in the examples on the right. In these examples there are no line numbers, so the computer carries out each instruction as soon as you press RETURN. It will print exactly what you typed between the quotation marks, including any spaces. The word PRINT by itself on a line tells the computer to leave an empty line.

```
PRINT 254
254
PRINT 999
999
PRINT

PRINT "*** ZEBRAS ***"
*** ZEBRAS ***
PRINT "RATS"
RATS
```


Doing calculations ▶

You can also use PRINT to display the answers to calculations. The computer uses the usual signs for adding and subtracting, but for multiplying it uses a * and for dividing a / sign. SQR(N) is the instruction for finding the square root of a number, N, and ↑ or ∧ or * * means to the power of. For example, $3 \uparrow 2$ means 3 to the power of 2, or 3 squared.

In complicated calculations the computer always works out multiplications and divisions before it adds or subtracts. To override this you can use brackets to tell the computer in which order to work out the sums. In calculations with lots of brackets, the computer works out the innermost brackets first.

```
PRINT 12095+277
12372
PRINT 239-51
188
PRINT 17*5
85
PRINT 221/13
17
```

```
PRINT SQR(9)
3
PRINT SQR(9)+3 ∧ 2
12
PRINT 2*17-5
29
PRINT 2*(17-5)
24
```

Commas and semi-colons ▶

These tell the computer where to print the next character on the screen. A semi-colon tells it not to leave any space and a comma tells it to move along a certain amount (the amount varies on different computers).

Some computers need a comma or semi-colon to separate PRINT statements and data or variables (letters representing pieces of data in the computer's memory). Try the examples on the right to see how they work on your computer.

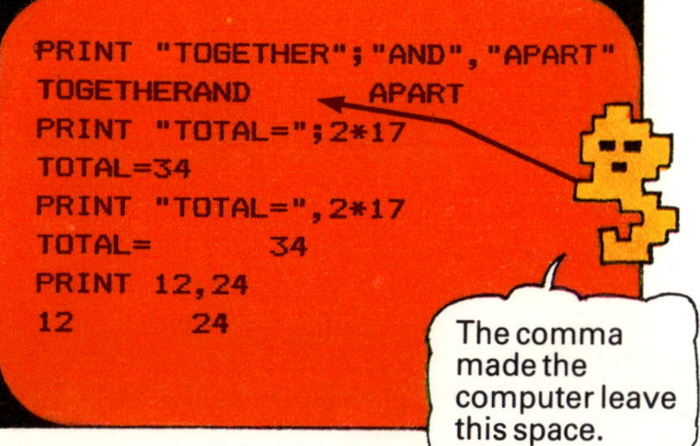

```
PRINT "TOGETHER";"AND","APART"
TOGETHERAND        APART
PRINT "TOTAL=";2*17
TOTAL=34
PRINT "TOTAL=",2*17
TOTAL=        34
PRINT 12,24
12        24
```

Variables ▶

Information which you give the computer to work on is called data. When you give the computer a piece of data to store in its memory you have to give it a label, too. The label is called a variable and when you want the computer to do something with the data you refer to it by its variable name. It is called a variable because the data to which it refers can change during the program.

You use letters of the alphabet, or a letter and a number, e.g. A6, as labels for number data. A piece of data consisting of letters and symbols is called a string and for strings you use a letter of the alphabet, or a letter and a number, with a dollar sign, e.g. P$ (pronounced P dollar or P string), or P6$. Different computers have different rules for variable names, so check in your computer manual.

LET ▶

This is one way to give the computer data. LET A=5 tells the computer to store the figure 5 in its memory and label it A and LET C$="RABBITS" stores the string of letters in a memory space labelled C$. Strings must always be in quotes but numbers do not need quotes.

INPUT ▶

This is a way of giving the computer data while the program is running. The word INPUT is followed by a variable name and when the computer reaches an INPUT command it prints a question mark (or other symbol) on the screen and waits for you to type in the data. If the INPUT variable is a number variable you must give it number data and if it is a string variable you must give it a string.

On most computers you can put words in quotes in an INPUT instruction to make it clearer, as shown in the second example on the right. Do not use this method on the VIC computer, though, as the VIC will store the words in the variable along with your input. Most computers need a semi-colon between the words and the variable name.

Most computers have special keys to delete characters typed by mistake. To correct a line in a program you can type the whole line again, including the line number. The new line will replace the line with the mistake. To delete a line altogether, type just the line number by itself.

READ/DATA ▶

This is another way of giving the computer data. The word READ is followed by one or several variable names and the data for the variables is in a line starting with the word DATA. The data line can be anywhere in the program. When the computer comes across the instruction READ it looks for the word DATA and then puts each data item in order into the variables. The data items must be separated by commas and with some computers, string data must be in quotes. Others need quotes only if the strings contain spaces or punctuation.

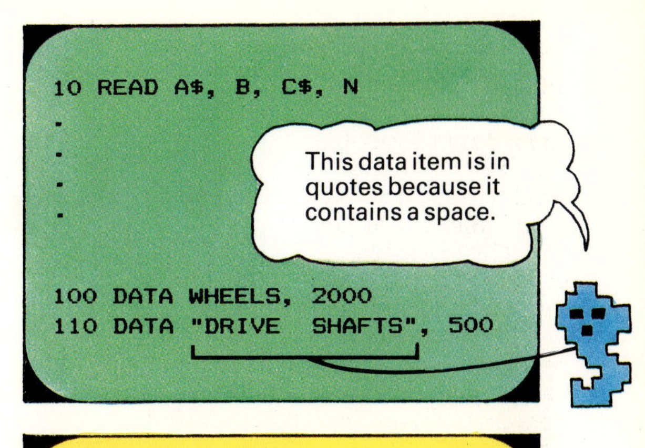

IF/THEN ▶

This is a way of testing data and telling the computer to do certain things depending on the result. You can test to see if two pieces of data are equal, not equal, or if one is greater than or less than the other, using the symbols shown on the right. Almost any instruction can follow the word THEN, but if the test is not true, the computer ignores the THEN and carries on with the rest of the program.

GOTO ▶

This tells the computer to go to another line in the program. It is usually used with IF/THEN so the computer branches only if certain conditions are true. Be careful when using GOTO by itself as it can make a continuous loop, as shown in line 185 on the right. The only way to stop this program running would be to type BREAK or ESCAPE (this command varies on different computers).

GOSUB/RETURN ▶

GOSUB makes the computer go to a subroutine, a special part of the program for carrying out a particular task. The word RETURN at the end of the subroutine sends the computer back to the instruction after the GOSUB command. You get a bug if you forget the word RETURN.

REM ▶

This is short for reminder, or remark. The computer ignores lines starting with the word REM and it is useful for inserting notes in the program to remind you what is happening.

7

FOR/NEXT loops ▶

The words FOR, TO and NEXT make the computer repeat part of a program a certain number of times. In the example on the right, lines 10 to 30 are repeated three times and each time the computer prints out the message in line 20. J is a variable to count the number of repeats. Line 30 sends the computer back to find the next value of J and each time the loop is repeated one is added to J. When J=3 the computer carries on with the rest of the program.

STEP ▶

This changes the way J counts the number of repeats. For example, FOR J=1 TO 10 STEP 2 makes J increase by 2 each time and STEP X would make it increase by whatever amount was stored in X. In the example on the right, STEP −1 makes J count backwards.

Nested loops ▶

You can make quite complicated repeats by using loops inside loops. These are called nested loops. For example, in the program on the right, each time the loop from lines 10 to 50 is repeated, the loop from lines 20 to 40 runs 12 times. Each time the inner loop is repeated, line 30 prints out the value of J×I.

Graphics commands ▶

The computer makes pictures by lighting up little squares, called pixels, on the screen. The instruction for lighting up pixels varies on different computers. The programs in this book use the instruction PLOT X,Y where X and Y are the co-ordinates of a pixel. To draw a line the programs use DRAW X,Y. Most computers have similar instructions, but some may need an extra instruction to tell them which graphics mode you want.*

RND ▶

This makes the computer produce a random number but the precise instruction varies on different computers. On some RND(9) produces a number between 1 and 9. Others need a more complicated instruction like this: INT(RND(1)*9+1). The computer works out everything in the brackets first. RND(1) makes it produce a number between 0 and 1. It multiplies this by 9, the highest number you want, then adds 1 because the word INT makes it a whole number by rounding down.

8

*Most computers have several different "modes" and in each mode they can work with different numbers of colours and pixels.

Arrays ▼

An array is a set of data items held together under one variable name. You could imagine the variable as a space in the computer's memory with lots of compartments. Arrays can be one-dimensional, that is, a single row of boxes, or two-dimensional and have several rows of boxes. You refer to an item in a one-dimensional array by the number of the box it is in, e.g. in the picture below A$(4) is PLUM. For two-dimensional arrays you have to give the number of the row and the column, e.g. D(3,2) is 15. The numbers in brackets are called subscripts.

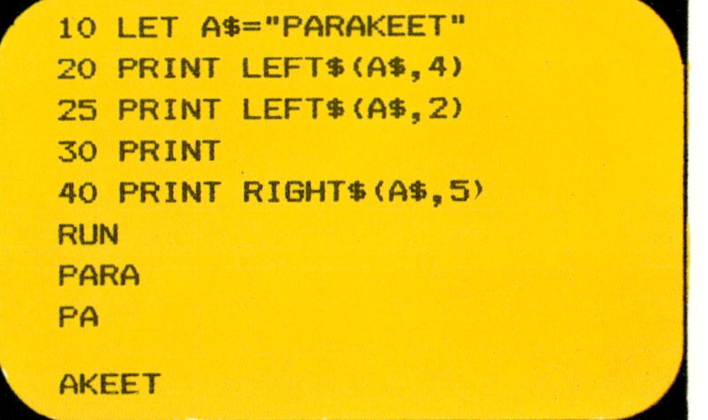

Before you use an array you have to tell the computer how big it will be using the word DIM (short for dimension) as shown on the right. To put the data in an array you use READ/DATA with a loop. For a two-dimensional array you need nested loops, as shown on the right.

    In this example I is the row number and J is the column number. Each time the inner loop J repeats, it puts a piece of data into the next column in the row. When the I loop repeats the computer starts a new row.

```
20 DIM D(4,3)
30 FOR I=1 TO 4
40 FOR J=1 TO 3
50 READ D(I,J)
60 NEXT J
70 NEXT I
80 DATA 5, 12, 16
90 DATA 3, 2, 7
100 DATA 8, 15, 11
110 DATA 4, 1, 7
```

LEFT$ and RIGHT$ ▶

These are for doing things with the characters held in string variables. For example, LEFT$(A$,4) tells the computer to take four characters from the left of A$ and RIGHT$(A$,5) means take five characters from the right. Sinclair computers do not use these commands. For the instructions to use on Sinclair computers see page 11.

```
10 LET A$="PARAKEET"
20 PRINT LEFT$(A$,4)
25 PRINT LEFT$(A$,2)
30 PRINT
40 PRINT RIGHT$(A$,5)
RUN
PARA
PA

AKEET
```

MID$ and LEN ▶

MID$ tells the computer to take some characters from the middle of a string and LEN tells you how many characters, including punctuation and spaces, there are in a string. For instance, MID$(K$,2,4) means take four characters from the middle of K$, starting with the second character. See page 11 for the instructions to use on Sinclair computers.

```
10 LET K$="TRAVESTY"
20 PRINT MID$(K$,2,4)
25 PRINT MID$(K$,4,4)
30 PRINT
35 PRINT LEN(K$)
RUN
RAVE
VEST

8
```

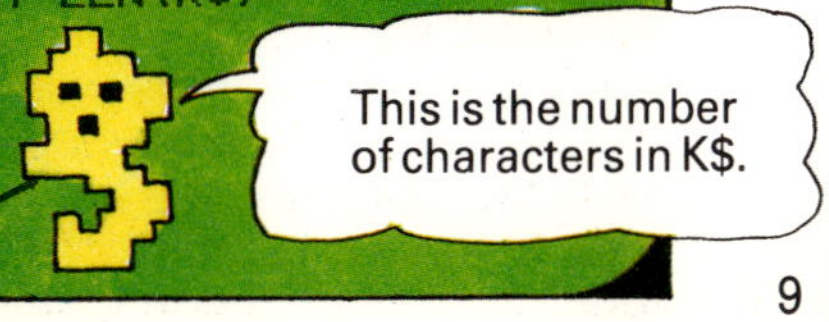

The BASIC in this book

The programs in this book are written in "standard" BASIC. Some computers, though, have their own special ways of doing things and you may have to make some minor changes to run the programs on your computer. On these two pages there are some points you should watch out for.

The programs are written to run on many different makes of computer so they do not take into account the special features of any one particular machine. Once you know how the programs work, though, you could adapt them so they make use of some of your computer's special features.

Variable names ▶

Some computers can use words as variable names and others will accept only letters, or letters and digits. For instance, on Sinclair computers you can use short words for number variables, but you are only allowed to use one letter for string variable names. In the programs in this book, most of the variables are labelled with words to make them easier to understand. If your computer does not accept words, use just the first letter of the word for the variable name.

LET ▶

Most computers do not need the word LET in a statement such as LET FRUIT$="APPLE". Some computers also do not need the THEN in IF . . . THEN statements. All the programs in this book use LET and THEN, but you can leave them out if your computer does not need them.

Initializing variables ▶

On some computers you have to set up, or initialize a variable before you can use it. This means you have to give the variable a value at the beginning of the program, as shown on the right. Others will assume a number variable is 0 and a string variable is empty without you initializing them. The programs in this book include lines to initialize the variables, but you can leave them out if your computer does not need them.

INPUT ▶

Most computers will accept words in quotes with an INPUT statement.* They vary, though, as to whether they need a semicolon before the INPUT variable and whether they automatically leave a space between the words and the data you input. You can find out what your computer needs by experimenting, or by looking in your manual.

```
100 FRUIT$="APPLE"
110 COUNT=COUNT+1
120 IF COUNT=10 PRINT "READY"
```

*Do not use this method on the VIC computer, though, as it will put the words in the variable as well as the data.

DATA

```
100 DATA MOUSE, GERBIL, RAT
110 DATA GNU, "THREE-TOED SLOTH"
120 DATA "DEER, RED", "RHINO, BLACK", GIRAFFE
```


Be especially careful typing in data lines. Each data item must be separated by a comma and it is very easy to make mistakes. Some computers also need their data words in quotes. Others only need quotation marks if the data includes spaces or punctuation.

Multiple statement lines

```
500   PLOT 40,1: DRAW 1,1

180   IF A=10 THEN PRINT "CORRECT": GOTO 100
```


Most computers will accept several instructions on the same line, separated by a colon as shown above. This uses less memory space and can make the program easier to read. If your computer does not accept multiple statement lines, put each instruction on a new line. If you are using multiple statement lines in your own programs, beware of putting extra statements after IF . . . THEN instructions as they will only be carried out if the IF condition is true.

RND and graphics commands

These commands vary on all computers. In the programs in this book the instruction to produce a random number between 1 and N (where N is any number), is INT(RND(1)*N+1). The graphics commands are PLOT X,Y for a point and DRAW X,Y for drawing a line. You will need to substitute your computer's commands for all of these. If your computer also needs a general graphics instruction you will need to insert this in the programs.

Sinclair computers and strings

Sinclair computers handle strings in a non-standard way. They do not use LEFT$, RIGHT$ or MID$. Instead you have to tell them exactly which characters to pick from a string. For example, on a Sinclair computer PRINT A$(1 TO 4) is the same as PRINT LEFT$(A$,4) and PRINT A$(4 TO 8) is the same as MID$(A$,4,5).

In string arrays, each string must have the same number of characters (you can pad out short strings with spaces) and each character of a string is stored in a separate compartment in the array. Some of the programs in this book need converting to run on Sinclair computers and the conversions are given on pages 46-47.

Changing the programs

Once you have got a program running on your computer, and you have an idea of how it works, you can change and adapt it by inputting different data or by adding sound and colour.

When you are changing a program, check each line very carefully. Make sure you have enough loops, but not too many, to read in the new data, and remember to change DIM statements, too.

Learning BASIC by studying programs

One good way to learn BASIC is to study other people's programs and see how they work. By studying the programs in this book you can see how to use loops and strings, how to write simple graphics programs and different ways of storing and sorting data. At first glance, some of the programs look really complicated. A complicated program, though, is only a long list of BASIC commands put together in an orderly way. On these two pages there are some tips and hints to help you study and understand programs.

Studying a program

Most programs are made up of several different parts (sometimes called routines or modules) for carrying out different tasks. For instance, in a rocket chase game one part of the program will be for plotting the rockets on the screen and other parts will register attacks and hits, keep track of fuel levels and speed and print out the final scores.

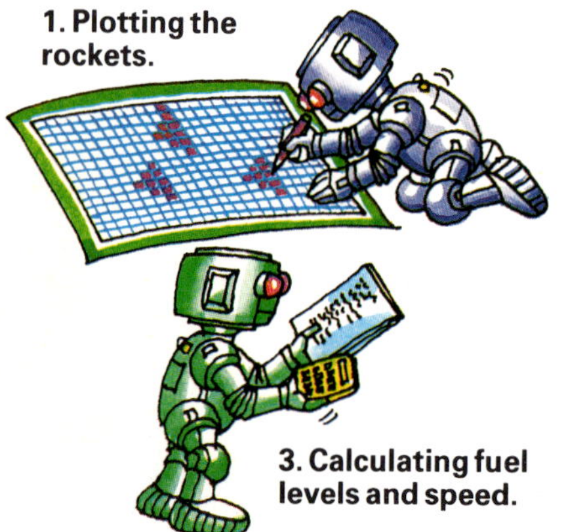

The first stage in studying a program is to try and recognize the different parts and work out what they are for. This gives you a general idea of how the program works. Look out for subroutines for carrying out particular tasks and for big jumps in the line numbers – lines starting at the next hundred or thousand often indicate a new part of the program. Sometimes the different parts of the program are labelled with REM statements.

Deciphering variables

Probably the most difficult thing to understand in the program is the variables. Before you type a program into a computer it is a good idea to work out the role of each variable and make a note of it. Certain variables are often used for the same tasks, so you can instantly recognize them. For instance, the letters I, J, K, L are usually used for loops and Z or Z$ is used for data that will only be needed for a short while.

Running and debugging programs

After working out what the variables are for, type the program into a computer. Since the programs are written in standard BASIC, you may have to change some of the BASIC commands to suit your computer.

Then try and run the program. There will probably be some bugs so list the program on the screen and look for typing errors or commands which are incorrect for your computer.

Once you have found all the bugs, run the program a few times to see how it works. It is a good idea to save it on a cassette or disk at this stage so you never have to type it in again.

Then turn back to the listing and study each line and try and work out what it does. Look out for short routines which you might be able to incorporate in your own programs.

You can use the computer to help you understand how the program works. Try altering the value of one of the variables and see how it affects the program. Make only one small change at a time so you can see what effect each change has. Remember to type in the correct figures again when you have finished.

You can also insert lines to print out the values of variables so you can see how they change during the program. You may find it useful to insert STOP commands, too, so you can study the program in stages, but remember to delete them afterwards. Some computers have a command CONTINUE which you can use after STOP.

Using strings

This program shows how you can combine quite simple BASIC commands to make the computer carry out complex tasks. The program is a word-spotting game in which the computer asks you for a word, then prints the letters randomly across the screen and asks you to spot how many times the word appears. It uses the string-handling commands MID$, RIGHT$ and LEN, and random numbers. *

There are two main tasks to carry out in the program. One is to print the letters randomly on the screen and the other is to get the computer to count the number of times the word occurs correctly.

```
WORD SPOTTING GAME
PLEASE TYPE IN A SHORT WORD
?CAKE
NOW SEE IF YOU CAN SPOT YOUR
WORD AS THE LETTERS APPEAR
ON THE SCREEN.
PRESS RETURN TO START
```

```
C K E K A E C A A K C K A E C
A K E C E A K C E A K C A K E
A C A E E C K K C C A E C A K
TYPE AS A FIGURE HOW MANY
TIMES YOU THINK YOUR WORD
APPEARED ON THE SCREEN ?1
WRONG!
YOUR WORD APPEARED 2 TIMES
```

Choosing the random letters

The program uses MID$ with a random number to choose which letters to print. Your word is stored in W$. At line 160 it picks a random number from 1 to the length of your word and stores it in R. Then in line 170 it uses the number in R to decide which letter to select from W$. It stores the letter in L$ and then prints it on the screen in line 180. Each time the loop from line 150 to 220 is repeated, a new number is stored in R and a new letter is chosen from W$.

Checking for the word

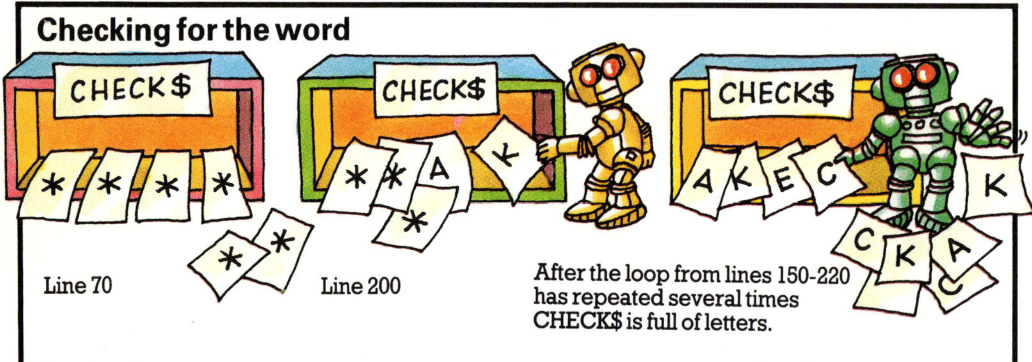

At the beginning of the program the computer sets aside a memory space called CHECK$ and fills it with the same number of stars as there are letters in your word. Each time it picks a new random letter it throws out the first character in CHECK$ and adds the random letter to the end of the string (line 200). Then, in line 210 it compares CHECK$ with W$ and if the letters are in the same order it adds 1 to N.

*To convert the program for Sinclair (Timex) computers see page 46.

Word spotting game

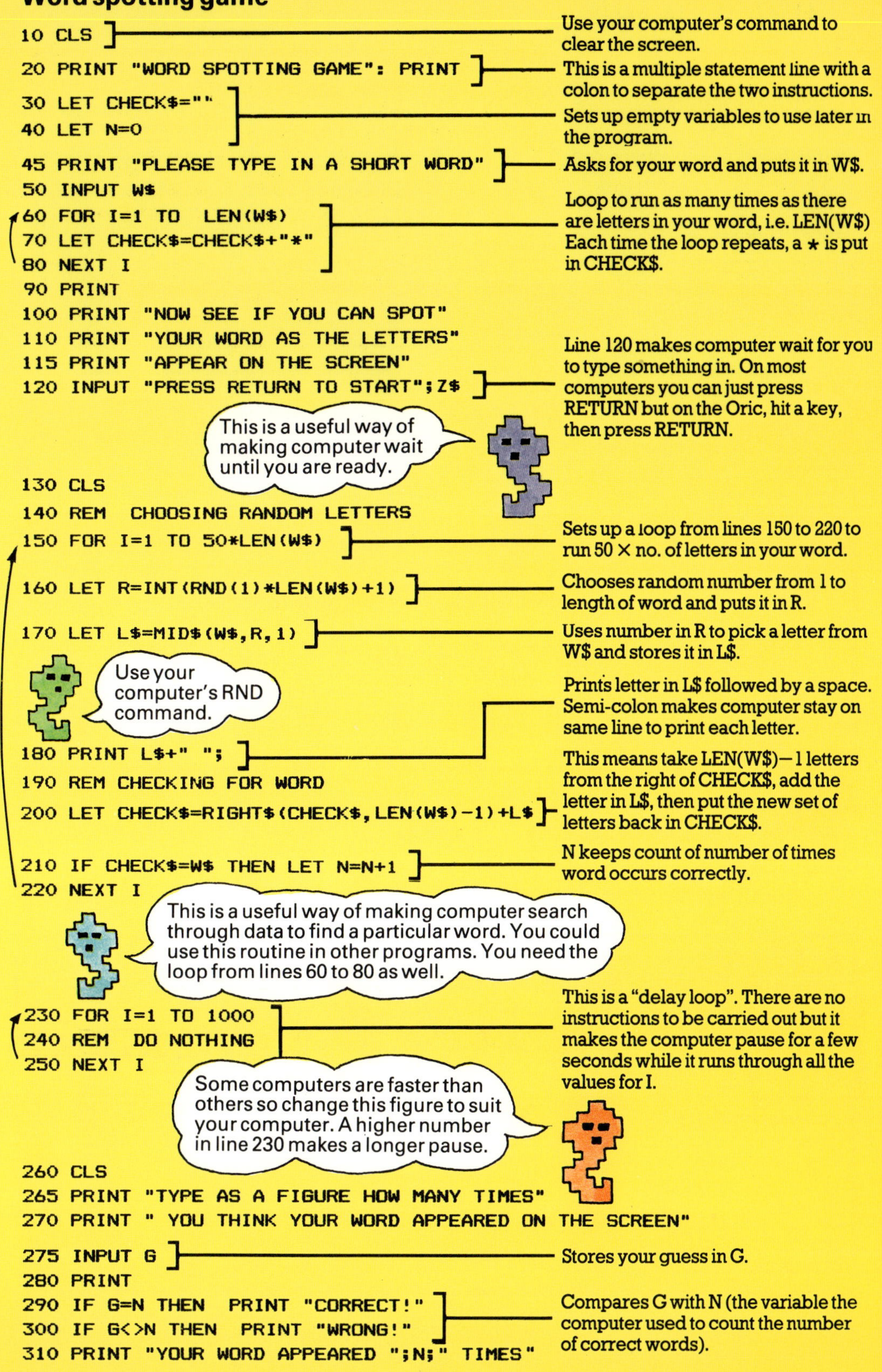


```
10 CLS
20 PRINT "WORD SPOTTING GAME": PRINT
30 LET CHECK$=""
40 LET N=0
45 PRINT "PLEASE TYPE IN A SHORT WORD"
50 INPUT W$
60 FOR I=1 TO  LEN(W$)
70 LET CHECK$=CHECK$+"*"
80 NEXT I
90 PRINT
100 PRINT "NOW SEE IF YOU CAN SPOT"
110 PRINT "YOUR WORD AS THE LETTERS"
115 PRINT "APPEAR ON THE SCREEN"
120 INPUT "PRESS RETURN TO START";Z$
130 CLS
140 REM   CHOOSING RANDOM LETTERS
150 FOR I=1 TO 50*LEN(W$)
160 LET R=INT(RND(1)*LEN(W$)+1)
170 LET L$=MID$(W$,R,1)
180 PRINT L$+" ";
190 REM CHECKING FOR WORD
200 LET CHECK$=RIGHT$(CHECK$,LEN(W$)-1)+L$
210 IF CHECK$=W$ THEN LET N=N+1
220 NEXT I
230 FOR I=1 TO 1000
240 REM   DO NOTHING
250 NEXT I
260 CLS
265 PRINT "TYPE AS A FIGURE HOW MANY TIMES"
270 PRINT " YOU THINK YOUR WORD APPEARED ON THE SCREEN"
275 INPUT G
280 PRINT
290 IF G=N THEN  PRINT "CORRECT!"
300 IF G<>N THEN  PRINT "WRONG!"
310 PRINT "YOUR WORD APPEARED ";N;" TIMES"
```

Use your computer's command to clear the screen.

This is a multiple statement line with a colon to separate the two instructions.

Sets up empty variables to use later in the program.

Asks for your word and puts it in W$.

Loop to run as many times as there are letters in your word, i.e. LEN(W$) Each time the loop repeats, a * is put in CHECK$.

Line 120 makes computer wait for you to type something in. On most computers you can just press RETURN but on the Oric, hit a key, then press RETURN.

Sets up a loop from lines 150 to 220 to run 50 × no. of letters in your word.

Chooses random number from 1 to length of word and puts it in R.

Uses number in R to pick a letter from W$ and stores it in L$.

Prints letter in L$ followed by a space. Semi-colon makes computer stay on same line to print each letter.

This means take LEN(W$)−1 letters from the right of CHECK$, add the letter in L$, then put the new set of letters back in CHECK$.

N keeps count of number of times word occurs correctly.

This is a "delay loop". There are no instructions to be carried out but it makes the computer pause for a few seconds while it runs through all the values for I.

Stores your guess in G.

Compares G with N (the variable the computer used to count the number of correct words).

15

Loops and random numbers

This program is a spacegame which also tests your mental arithmetic. It shows some of the ways in which you can use loops and random numbers and there are some special screen effects which you could incorporate in your own programs. It is quite a long program, but most of the lines are PRINT statements to set the scene for the game.

Spaceflight emergency game

```
100 CLS
110 FOR I=1 TO 20
115 PRINT "**** WARNING **";
118 PRINT "** RED ALERT ****";
120 FOR J=1 TO 10
125 REM DO NOTHING
130 NEXT J
135 NEXT I
140 CLS
150 FOR I=1 TO 20
155 PRINT "**** CIRCUIT DAMAGE ****";
160 FOR J=1 TO 10
165 REM DO NOTHING
170 NEXT J
180 NEXT I
190 CLS
200 PRINT "THIS IS YOUR SHIP'S COMPUTER
SPEAKING ..."
210 PRINT
220 PRINT "WE ARE IN TROUBLE.  I CANNOT
CALCULATE FUEL FEED RATES."
230 PRINT
240 PRINT "AS WE APPROACH EARTH, YOU WILL
HAVE TO DO THE CALCULATIONS."
250 PRINT
260 PRINT "I CAN TELL YOU HOW MUCH FUEL
WE NEED AT EACH STAGE, AND THE TIME PERIOD
IN WHICH IT MUST BE USED."
270 PRINT
280 PRINT "YOU MUST DIVIDE THE FUEL BY
THE TIME TO GIVE ME THE RATE AT WHICH
THE SHIP MUST BURN THE FUEL."
290 PRINT
300 PRINT "HERE IS AN EXAMPLE"
310 PRINT "------------------"
320 PRINT "FUEL=24"
330 PRINT "TIME=6"
345 PRINT
350 INPUT "PLEASE DIVIDE FUEL BY TIME AND
TYPE IN THE ANSWER QUICKLY ";ANSWER
360 PRINT
370 IF ANSWER<>4 THEN  PRINT "NO. TRY
AGAIN, YOUR LIFE DEPENDS ON IT": GOTO 350
380 CLS
```

Use your computer's command to clear the screen.

Lines 110 to 135 are nested loops. Each time the I loop is carried out the warning in lines 115-118 is printed, then the J loop repeats ten times. The J loop is a delay loop to make the computer pause a moment so you can read the warning.

Lines 150-180 work like lines 110-135.

The next part of the program prints a description of the game on the screen. If the sentences are too long for your screen insert extra PRINT lines.

PRINT by itself leaves empty lines.

Underlines words in the line above.

Your reply is stored in ANSWER.

The GOTO is carried out only if ANSWER is not 4. (If your computer does not use multiple statement lines, repeat IF ... THEN on a new line with GOTO.)

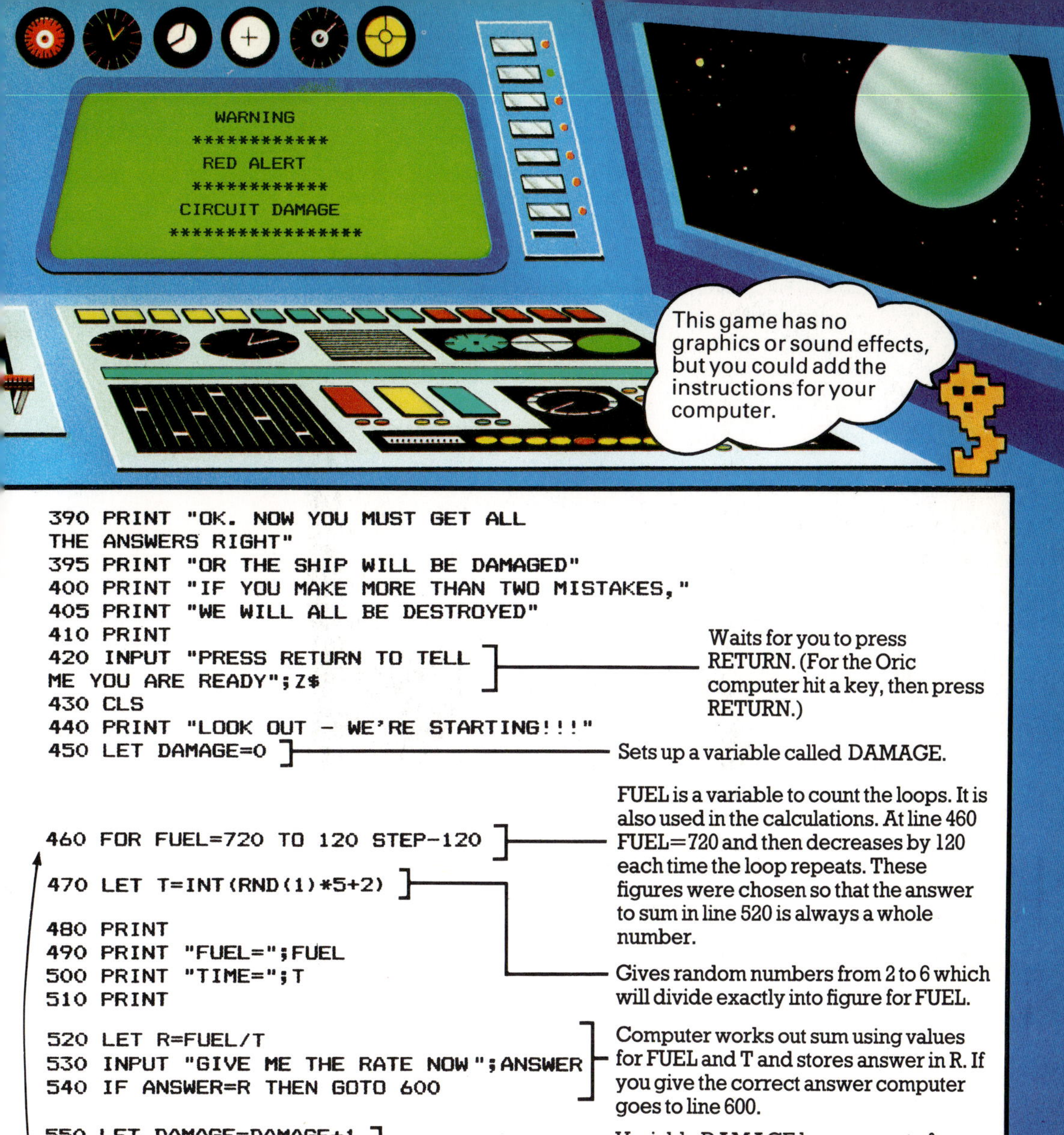


```
390 PRINT "OK. NOW YOU MUST GET ALL
THE ANSWERS RIGHT"
395 PRINT "OR THE SHIP WILL BE DAMAGED"
400 PRINT "IF YOU MAKE MORE THAN TWO MISTAKES,"
405 PRINT "WE WILL ALL BE DESTROYED"
410 PRINT
420 INPUT "PRESS RETURN TO TELL
ME YOU ARE READY";Z$
430 CLS
440 PRINT "LOOK OUT - WE'RE STARTING!!!"
450 LET DAMAGE=0

460 FOR FUEL=720 TO 120 STEP-120
470 LET T=INT(RND(1)*5+2)
480 PRINT
490 PRINT "FUEL=";FUEL
500 PRINT "TIME=";T
510 PRINT
520 LET R=FUEL/T
530 INPUT "GIVE ME THE RATE NOW ";ANSWER
540 IF ANSWER=R THEN GOTO 600
550 LET DAMAGE=DAMAGE+1
560 PRINT
570 PRINT "****DAMAGE****"
580 PRINT
590 IF DAMAGE>2 THEN GOTO 640
600 NEXT FUEL
610 CLS
620 PRINT "CONGRATULATIONS - YOU HAVE
DONE JUST AS WELL AS I COULD. YOU HAVE
REACHED EARTH SAFELY!!!"
630 GOTO 720
640 CLS
650 FOR I=1 TO 20
660 PRINT "*";
670 FOR J=1 TO INT(RND(1)*I+50)
680 PRINT "    ";
690 NEXT J
700 NEXT I
710 PRINT: PRINT "THE SHIP IS DESTROYED"
720 END
```

Waits for you to press RETURN. (For the Oric computer hit a key, then press RETURN.)

Sets up a variable called DAMAGE.

FUEL is a variable to count the loops. It is also used in the calculations. At line 460 FUEL=720 and then decreases by 120 each time the loop repeats. These figures were chosen so that the answer to sum in line 520 is always a whole number.

Gives random numbers from 2 to 6 which will divide exactly into figure for FUEL.

Computer works out sum using values for FUEL and T and stores answer in R. If you give the correct answer computer goes to line 600.

Variable DAMAGE keeps count of your mistakes.

If you make more than two mistakes the computer jumps out of the loop and goes to line 640.

Only prints this line if you make less than two mistakes.

These nested loops print a random pattern of stars on the screen. Each time the I loop repeats, the computer prints a star and then the J loop makes it leave a random number of spaces.

Making a soccer database

A database is a large amount of information stored in a computer. The information is organized so that the computer can combine and compare the facts and figures in various different ways and a person using the database can receive useful information in a very short time.

On the next few pages there is a program for a soccer World Cup database. This is an example of a small database which you can use to find out which team won the Cup in any year since 1930, or in which year a particular team won the Cup. At the end of the program there are some ideas for converting the database to hold different information, such as a magazine index or the data for a nature survey.

There are three main parts to a database program. You need a suitable way of storing the information, a means of retrieving it and a "menu". A menu is a list of the various things a program can do, from which you can choose what you want. The program should also be "user-friendly", that is, it should give the person using the database clear instructions, and should not "crash", or break down, if they make a mistake.

Sample database runs

Storing the information

	1930	1934	1938	1950	1954	1958	1962	1966	1970	1974	1978	1982
URUGUAY	1	0	0	1	0	0	0	0	0	0	0	0
ARGENTINA	2	0	0	0	0	0	0	0	0	0	1	0
ITALY	0	1	1	0	0	0	0	0	2	0	0	1
CZECHOSLOVAKIA	0	2	0	0	0	0	2	0	0	0	0	0
HUNGARY	0	0	2	0	2	0	0	0	0	0	0	0
WEST GERMANY	0	0	0	0	1	0	0	2	0	1	0	2
BRAZIL	0	0	0	0	0	1	1	0	1	0	0	0
SWEDEN	0	0	0	0	0	2	0	0	0	0	0	0
ENGLAND	0	0	0	0	0	0	0	1	0	0	0	0
HOLLAND	0	0	0	0	0	0	0	0	0	2	2	0

To match the teams and years the program uses a "matrix" of information and looks up a team or year in the same way as you would on this chart. In the chart a figure 1 shows that a team won the Cup and a 2 shows that it was a finalist. By reading along the rows and down the columns you can see which team won in which year. The program is an automatic way of doing this, and of course, with large amounts of information, it is much quicker than a chart.

Building the matrix

It is quite easy to make a computer version of the chart on the opposite page using arrays. An array is a variable which can hold lots of separate items of data.

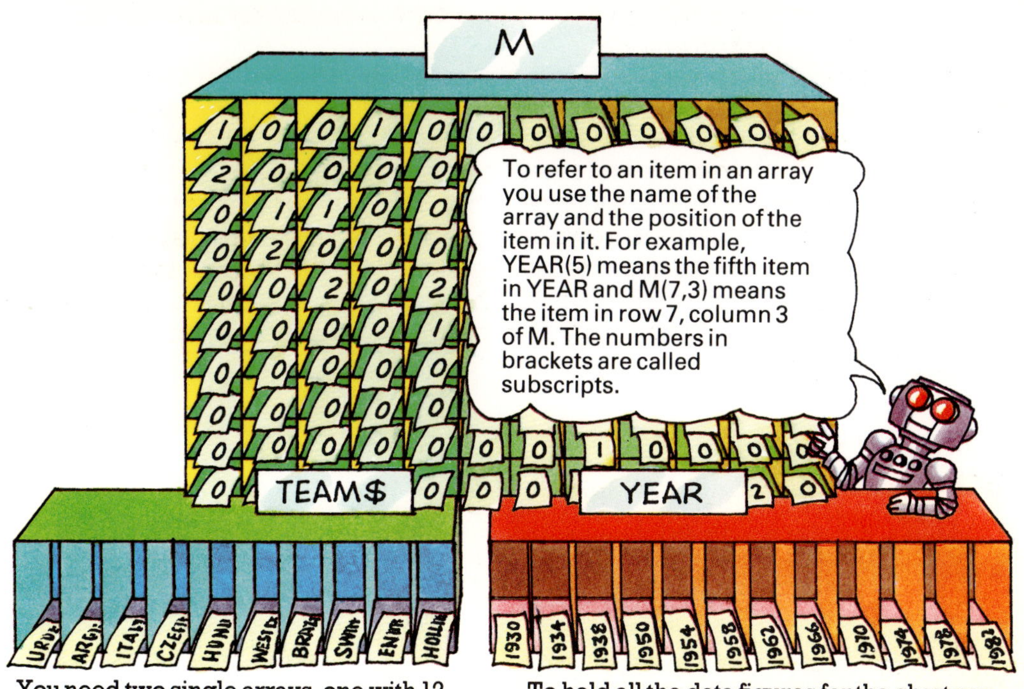

You need two single arrays, one with 12 compartments to hold the list of years and one with 10 to hold the teams. These are called YEAR and TEAM$ in the program.

To hold all the data figures for the chart you need a two-dimensional array with 10 rows and 12 columns. This is called M (for matrix) in the program.

How the computer uses the matrix

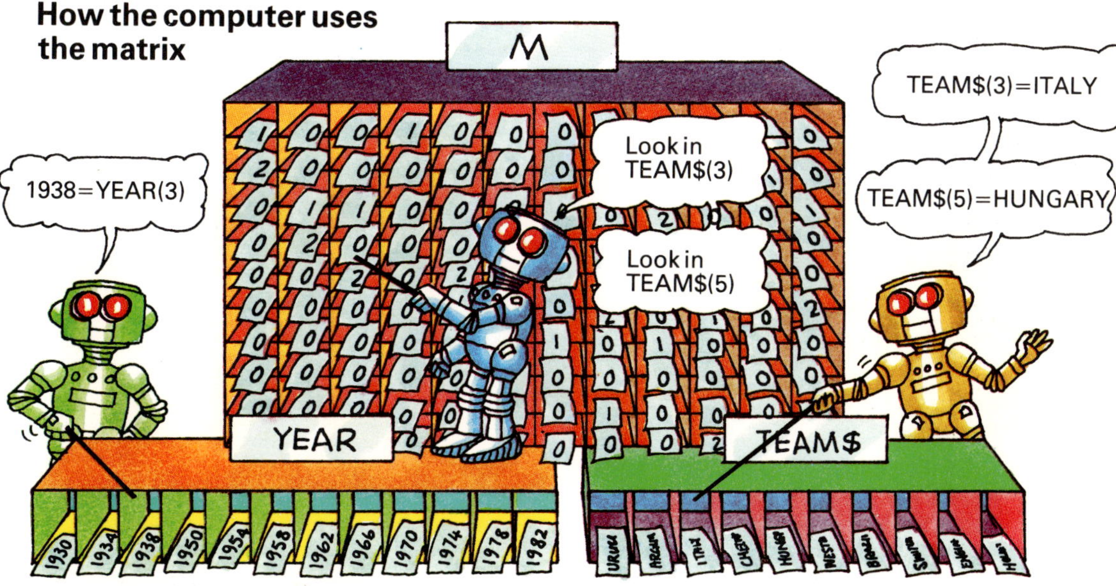

To find which team won the World Cup in, say, 1938, the computer looks for 1938 in the YEAR array and notes that it is in compartment 3. Then it looks through column 3 of the matrix and when it finds a 1 or 2 it notes the row number and uses this number to look up the name of the team in TEAM$.

The database program

There are seven main parts to the program, and each part is dealt with in a separate subroutine. The first few lines tell the computer which subroutine to use and after carrying out a subroutine it returns to these lines.

The subroutines starting at lines 200 and 300 are for printing out the list of teams and years. Lines 400-500 are for finding out in which year a particular team won the Cup, while lines 500-600 are for finding out which team won the Cup in a particular year. All the data is listed towards the end of the program, followed by the menu. It is usually best to put the data towards the end of the program, and keep the working part of the program at the beginning.

The menu

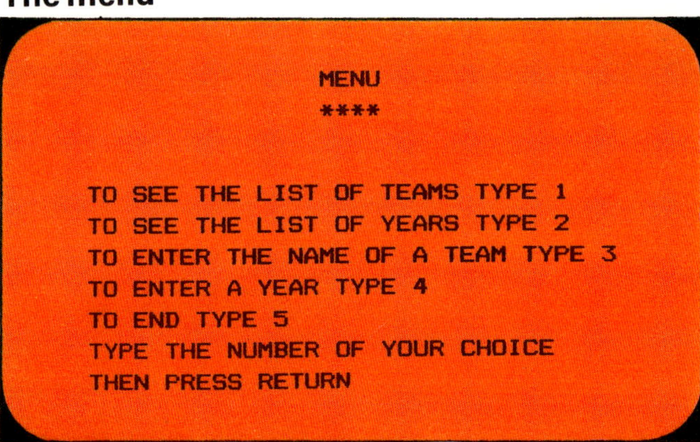

The menu is the part of the program which tells you what the program can do, and how to use it. In this program, you choose what you want by typing in a number. The number is stored in a variable C and the computer uses this number to call up the correct subroutine for carrying out the task you want.

Calling up the subroutines

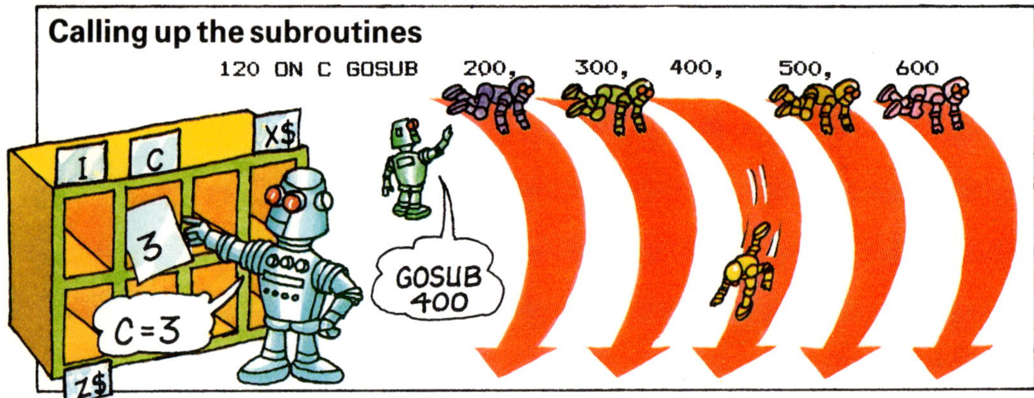

Line 120 in the program controls which subroutine the computer uses. The letter C is the variable which contains the number you typed in after seeing the menu. The computer uses the number in C to decide which subroutine to go to. If C=1 it goes to the first subroutine listed in line 120, i.e. the one starting at line 200. If C=2 it goes to the second, i.e. line 300. If C=3 it goes to the third, etc. ON GOSUB is a useful BASIC command to make the computer go to different subroutines depending on some test. If your computer does not have the command ON, you can use several IF . . . THEN statements instead, e.g. IF C=1 THEN GOSUB 200.

What the variables are for

YEAR	TEAM$	M
The array to hold the years.	The array to hold the names of the teams.	The two-dimensional array to hold all the data figures.

C	Z$	X$
The variable to hold the number you type in after seeing the menu.	The name of the team or year you type in.	Temporary data.

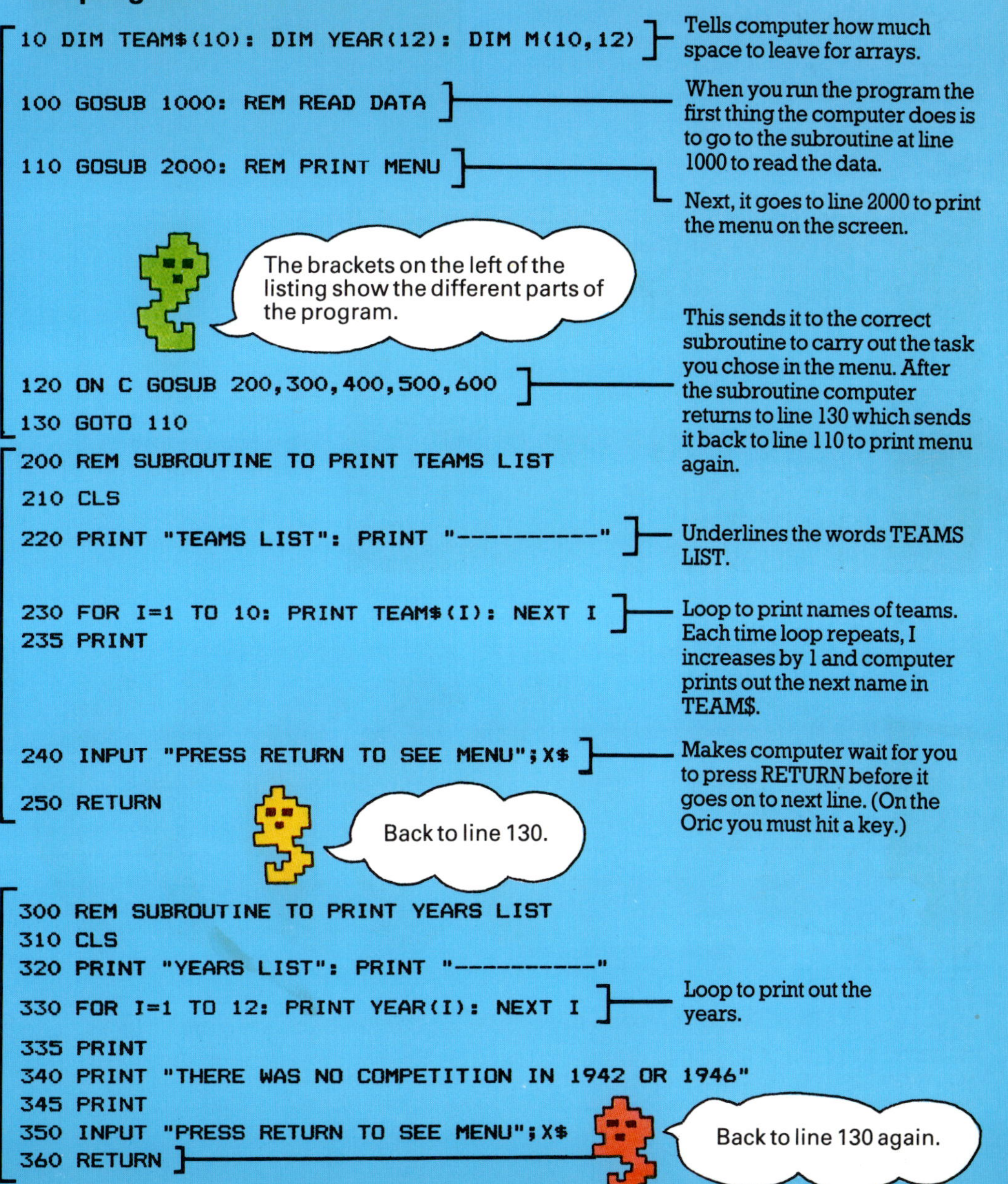

The program*

```
10 DIM TEAM$(10): DIM YEAR(12): DIM M(10,12)
```
Tells computer how much space to leave for arrays.

```
100 GOSUB 1000: REM READ DATA
```
When you run the program the first thing the computer does is to go to the subroutine at line 1000 to read the data.

```
110 GOSUB 2000: REM PRINT MENU
```
Next, it goes to line 2000 to print the menu on the screen.

```
120 ON C GOSUB 200,300,400,500,600
130 GOTO 110
```
This sends it to the correct subroutine to carry out the task you chose in the menu. After the subroutine computer returns to line 130 which sends it back to line 110 to print menu again.

```
200 REM SUBROUTINE TO PRINT TEAMS LIST
210 CLS
220 PRINT "TEAMS LIST": PRINT "----------"
```
Underlines the words TEAMS LIST.

```
230 FOR I=1 TO 10: PRINT TEAM$(I): NEXT I
235 PRINT
```
Loop to print names of teams. Each time loop repeats, I increases by 1 and computer prints out the next name in TEAM$.

```
240 INPUT "PRESS RETURN TO SEE MENU";X$
250 RETURN
```
Makes computer wait for you to press RETURN before it goes on to next line. (On the Oric you must hit a key.)

```
300 REM SUBROUTINE TO PRINT YEARS LIST
310 CLS
320 PRINT "YEARS LIST": PRINT "----------"
330 FOR I=1 TO 12: PRINT YEAR(I): NEXT I
```
Loop to print out the years.

```
335 PRINT
340 PRINT "THERE WAS NO COMPETITION IN 1942 OR 1946"
345 PRINT
350 INPUT "PRESS RETURN TO SEE MENU";X$
360 RETURN
```


*To convert this program to run on Sinclair (Timex) computers see page 46.

```
400 REM SUBROUTINE TO INPUT TEAM
405 CLS
410 INPUT "PLEASE TYPE IN THE NAME OF THE
TEAM, OR TYPE MENU TO SEE THE LIST AGAIN ";Z$
```
The name of a team or the word "menu" is stored in Z$.

```
415 IF Z$="MENU" THEN RETURN
```
If Z$=MENU computer returns to line 130 and from there to line 110 to print the menu.

```
420 FOR I=1 TO 10
425 IF Z$=TEAM$(I) THEN GOTO 440
430 NEXT I
```
Loop to compare Z$ with each name in TEAM$. When it finds a name which equals Z$ it goes to line 440.

```
435 PRINT: PRINT "TEAM NOT FOUND - PLEASE
TRY AGAIN": PRINT: GOTO 410
```
This line is a safeguard in case you misspell the name of a team, or type in a name not in the database.

```
440 PRINT
445 PRINT Z$: PRINT
```
Prints the name of the team.

Loop to make computer find details for your team in the matrix. I is the row number. The value for I is set by the loop at lines 420-430 and it is the subscript (the number which shows its position in the array) for your team in TEAM$. J is the column number and each time the loop repeats the computer looks in the next column along row I.

```
450 FOR J=1 TO 12
455 IF M(I,J)=1 THEN PRINT "WON THE WORLD
CUP IN  ";YEAR(J):PRINT
460 IF M(I,J)=2 THEN PRINT "WAS A FINALIST
IN ";YEAR(J): PRINT
465 NEXT J
```

```
470 PRINT
480 INPUT "PRESS RETURN FOR MENU";X$
```
Same as line 240.

```
490 RETURN
```



```
500 REM SUBROUTINE TO INPUT YEAR
505 CLS
510 INPUT "PLEASE TYPE IN THE YEAR, OR
TYPE MENU TO SEE THE LIST AGAIN ";Z$
```
Same as line 410, but this time your year is held in Z$.

```
515 IF Z$="MENU" THEN RETURN
520 FOR I=1 TO 12
525 IF VAL(Z$)=YEAR(I) THEN GOTO 540
530 NEXT I
```
Loop to compare Z$ with each of the years in YEAR. You cannot compare a string variable with a number variable, though, so you need the BASIC command VAL. This tells the computer to treat the characters in Z$ as a number.

```
535 PRINT: PRINT "YEAR NOT FOUND - TRY
AGAIN": PRINT: GOTO 510
```

```basic
540 PRINT: PRINT "IN ";Z$: PRINT
550 FOR J=1 TO 10
555 IF M(J,I)=1 THEN PRINT TEAM$(J);" WON
THE CUP"
560 NEXT J
565 PRINT
570 INPUT "PRESS RETURN FOR MENU";X$
580 RETURN
```

This loop works in the same way as lines 450-460. This time the column number is set by the subscript of the year in YEAR and the row number changes each time the loop repeats.


```basic
600 REM SUBROUTINE TO END PROGRAM
610 INPUT "END - SURE (Y/N)";X$
620 IF X$<>"Y" THEN RETURN ELSE END
```

Checks to make sure you want to stop. If you type Y the BASIC command END tells the computer to stop running the program. If you type anything else, it goes back to line 130. The word ELSE is a useful way of adding more conditions to IF . . . THEN statements. For more about this, see over the page.


```basic
1000 FOR I=1 TO 12: READ YEAR(I): NEXT I
1010 DATA 1930,1934,1938,1950
1020 DATA 1954, 1958, 1962, 1966
1030 DATA 1970, 1974, 1978, 1982
```

Loop to read the data into YEAR.

```basic
1100 FOR I=1 TO 10: READ TEAM$(I): NEXT I
1110 DATA URUGUAY, ARGENTINA
1115 DATA ITALY, CZECHOSLOVAKIA, HUNGARY
1120 DATA WEST GERMANY, BRAZIL
1125 DATA SWEDEN, ENGLAND, HOLLAND
```

Loop to read the data into TEAM$.


```basic
1200 FOR I=1 TO 10: FOR J=1 TO 12
1205 READ M(I,J)
1210 NEXT J: NEXT I

1215 RETURN
```

Nested loops to read data into the two dimensional array M.


```basic
1220 DATA 1,0,0,1,0,0,0,0,0,0,0,0
1230 DATA 2,0,0,0,0,0,0,0,0,0,1,0
1240 DATA 0,1,1,0,0,0,0,0,2,0,0,1
1250 DATA 0,2,0,0,0,0,2,0,0,0,0,0
1260 DATA 0,0,2,0,2,0,0,0,0,0,0,0
1270 DATA 0,0,0,0,1,0,0,2,0,1,0,2
1280 DATA 0,0,0,0,0,1,1,0,1,0,0,0
1290 DATA 0,0,0,0,0,2,0,0,0,0,0,0
1300 DATA 0,0,0,0,0,0,0,1,0,0,0,0
1310 DATA 0,0,0,0,0,0,0,0,0,0,2,2,0
```

This is the data for M.

LISTING CONTINUED OVER THE PAGE

```
2000 REM SUBROUTINE TO PRINT MENU

2010 CLS

2020 PRINT "              MENU"

2030 PRINT "              ****"

2040 FOR I=1 TO 6: PRINT: NEXT I

2050 PRINT "TO SEE THE LIST OF TEAMS TYPE 1"

2060 PRINT

2070 PRINT "TO SEE THE LIST OF YEARS TYPE 2"

2080 PRINT

2090 PRINT "TO ENTER THE NAME OF A TEAM TYPE 3"

2100 PRINT

2110 PRINT "TO ENTER A YEAR TYPE 4"

2120 PRINT

2130 PRINT "TO END TYPE 5"

2140 PRINT

2150 PRINT "TYPE THE NUMBER OF YOUR CHOICE"

2160 INPUT "THEN PRESS RETURN ";C

2170 IF C<1 OR C>5 THEN PRINT "PLEASE ENTER
A FIGURE BETWEEN 1 AND 5": GOTO 2150

2180 RETURN
```

Leave about 15 spaces here to centre the word menu above the list of choices.

Loop to leave six empty lines.

The number of your choice is stored in C.

This line is a safeguard in case you type in something other than a number between 1 and 5. For more about OR see below.

AND, OR and ELSE*

```
IF A=3 AND C$="YES" THEN LET D=D+1

IF X<0 OR X>100 THEN PRINT "OUT OF RANGE"

IF AGE<36 THEN PRINT "YOUNG" ELSE
PRINT "OLD"
```

You can use these BASIC words to add more tests and instructions to IF . . . THEN statements, as shown in the examples above. When you use AND the computer will carry out the THEN instruction only if both the tests in the IF statement are true. OR tells it to carry out the instruction if either of the tests are true. The word ELSE enables you to give the computer instructions to carry out if none of the tests are true. Can you write a short program using ELSE to solve the problem on the right?

Puzzle

Champion robot runner, Zak, can run 500 metres a second. If the temperature goes above or below 60° though, Zak speeds up or slows down by 10 metres a second. Can you write a program to print out how far Zak can run depending on the temperature and number of seconds you input? (Answer page 48.)

24

*These BASIC words are not available on all computers.

Converting the database

Once you understand how the program works it is quite easy to convert it to make a database for a different subject. There are some ideas for different databases below.

When you have decided on a subject for the database, draw up a chart with all the figures for the data, like the one on page 18. Your chart may have a different number of rows and columns, in which case you will need to change the size of the arrays in the program. Then put all your data in the data lines in the program, and rewrite the questions in the menu, too. Remember to change the DIM statements and the number of times the loops run to read the data into the arrays.

Magazine database

You could use a magazine database to see which month a subject appeared, or which subjects were covered in any one month. This could save hours skimming through magazines looking for a particular article. You would need an array called WEEK$ and another called SUBJECT$, as well as the matrix.

Wildlife database

A database of birds or plants could show either when, or where you spotted them. You would need one array for the names of the birds or plants and another for the place or time of year when you spotted them. Wildlife organizations are compiling databases like this to keep a record of the distribution of different species.

Food and vitamins database

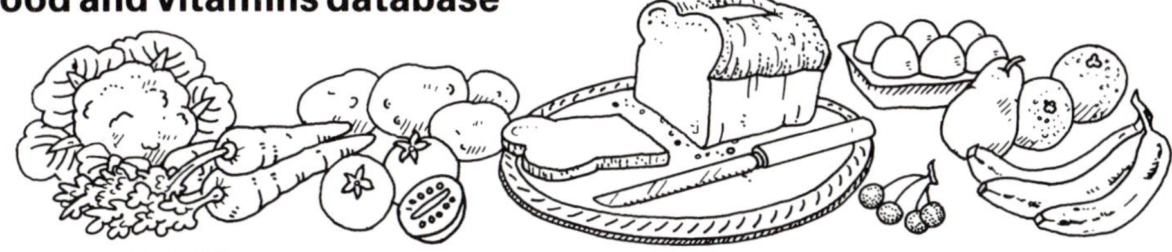

This database would enable you to find out which foods contained a certain vitamin, or which vitamins are present in a particular food. Another idea would be a foods and calories database, so you could see how many calories there are in a particular food, or which foods have more than a certain number of calories.

Instant graphics

This program draws simple shapes on the screen and fills them with a criss-cross grid of lines. Grids are often used in computer graphics to help make shapes look more three-dimensional or give them a space-age look.

The program uses the graphics command PLOT X, Y for plotting a point and DRAW X, Y for drawing a line. The co-ordinates X and Y are measured from the edge of the screen. You will have to convert these instructions for your computer, and add any special graphics commands that your computer may need. *

There are two different ways of writing graphics programs. You can tell the computer to calculate and plot all the points as it goes along and build up the picture gradually on the screen. Or you can make it do all the calculations first, store them in arrays, then plot the complete picture almost instantly. The following program uses the "instant graphics" approach.

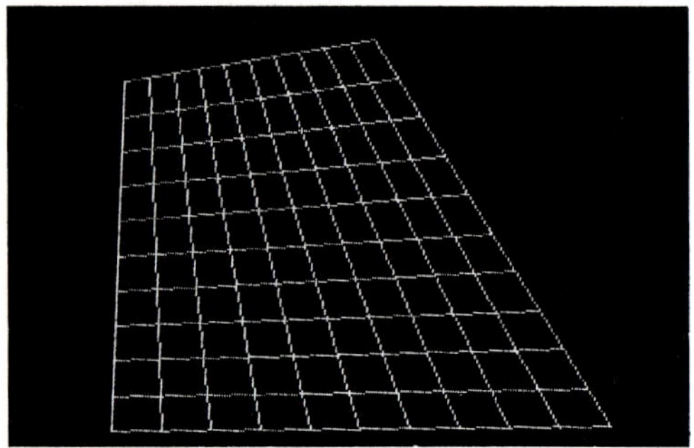

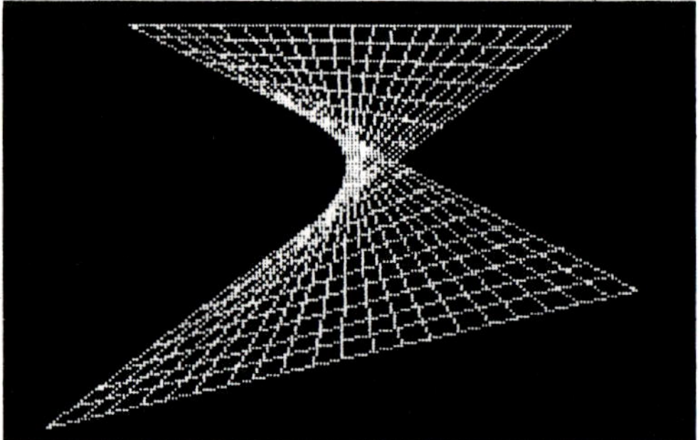

You can make all kinds of shapes and patterns by changing the data in the program. You can also draw the grid lines in different colours. There are some hints for adapting the program at the end of the listing.

There are three main parts to the program. The first part (lines 100-190) plots the corners of the grid and draws lines between them. The second part (lines 200-360) works out the co-ordinates for the grid lines and the third part (line 400-550) draws the lines.

The program uses four arrays for storing all the data for the co-ordinates. CX and CY hold the X and Y co-ordinates for the four corners of the grid. You give the computer the data for these arrays at the beginning of the program. CX(1) and CY(1) contain the co-ordinates for the first corner of the grid, CX(2) and CY(2) for the second, and so on.

*On some computers, e.g. Spectrum and the Oric, the X and Y co-ordinates for a line are measured from the last point plotted. To convert the program for these computers see page 47.

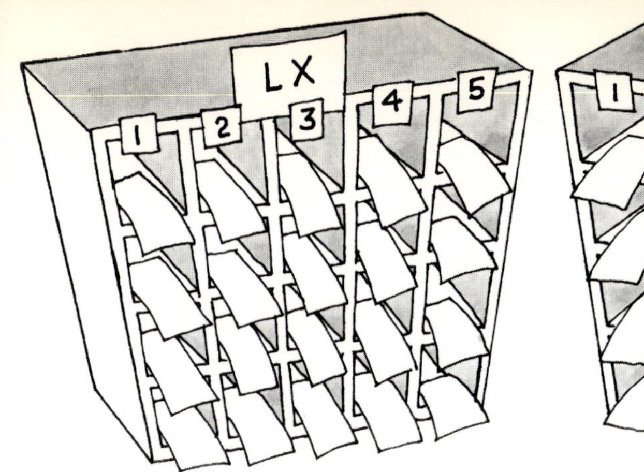

LX and LY are the arrays for holding the X and Y co-ordinates for the grid lines. They are two-dimensional arrays and they each have four rows. The number of columns is set in the program by the number of grid lines you want. Each row holds the co-ordinates for the lines for one side of the grid and row 1 equals side 1, etc. The computer stores the data in LX and LY as it works out the calculations in the program.

The program

```
100 INPUT "HOW MANY GRID LINES
DO YOU WANT? ";N
110 DIM CX(4),CY(4)
115 DIM LX(4,N), LY(4,N)
120 CLS
130 REM DRAW SIDES OF GRID
135 REM INSERT YOUR COMPUTER'S
GRAPHICS MODE INSTRUCTION
140 FOR I=1 TO 4
145 READ CX(I), CY(I)
150 NEXT I

160 DATA 100,50,700,50,500,700,150,500

170 PLOT CX(4),CY(4)

180 FOR I=1 TO 4
185 DRAW CX(I), CY(I)
190 NEXT I
```

Try 20 for computers with hi-res graphics and 5 for low-res.

Tells the computer how big to make the arrays.

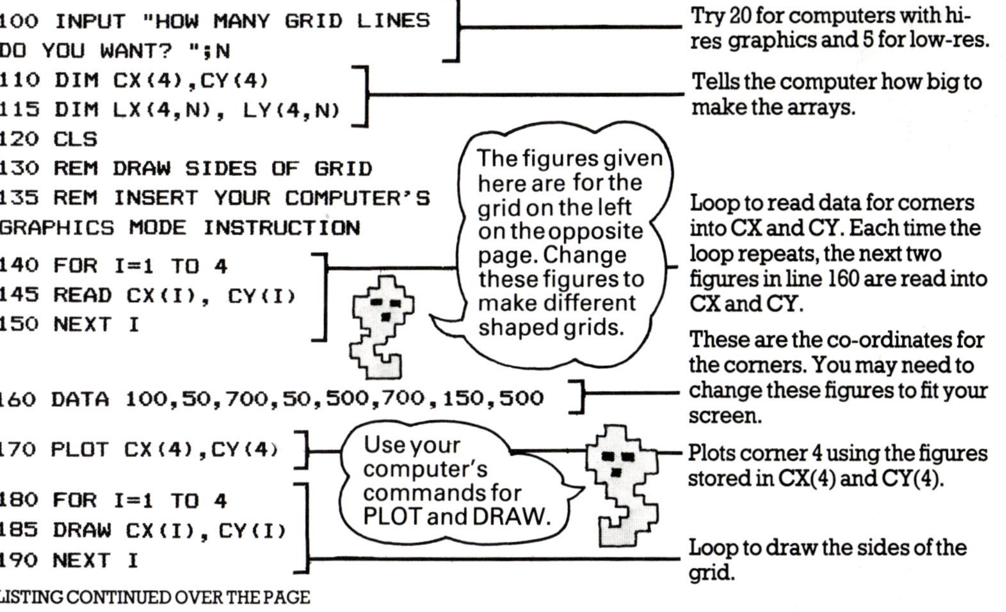

Loop to read data for corners into CX and CY. Each time the loop repeats, the next two figures in line 160 are read into CX and CY.

These are the co-ordinates for the corners. You may need to change these figures to fit your screen.

Plots corner 4 using the figures stored in CX(4) and CY(4).

Loop to draw the sides of the grid.

LISTING CONTINUED OVER THE PAGE

Drawing the sides

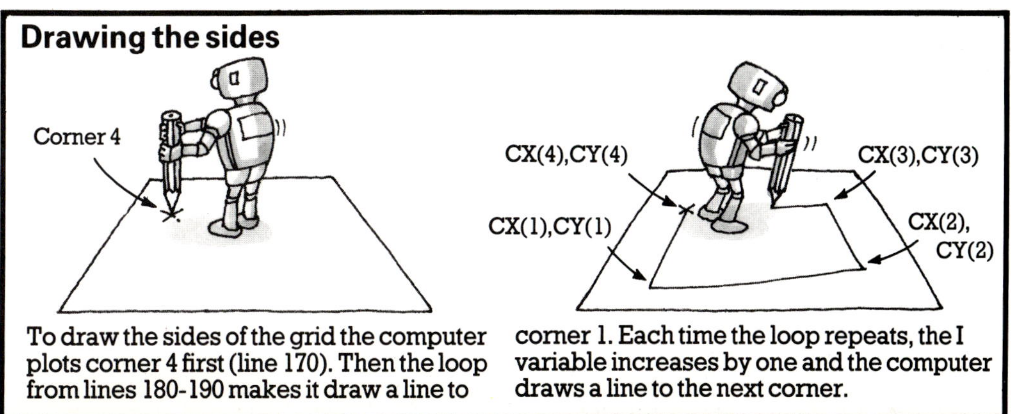

To draw the sides of the grid the computer plots corner 4 first (line 170). Then the loop from lines 180-190 makes it draw a line to corner 1. Each time the loop repeats, the I variable increases by one and the computer draws a line to the next corner.

```
200 REM CALCULATE CO-ORDINATES FOR GRID LINES
```

The next part of the program consists of four loops to calculate the co-ordinates for the grid lines. You can find out how in the pictures below.

```
210 FOR I=1 TO N
```

N is the number of grid lines you chose.

```
220 LET LX(1,I)=CX(1)+(CX(2)-CX(1))*I/N
```

Works out X co-ordinates for grid lines along side 1 and stores them in LX row 1, columns 1 to N.

```
230 LET LY(1,I)=CY(1)+(CY(2)-CY(1))*I/N
```

Works out Y co-ordinates for side 1 and stores them in LY row 1 columns 1 to N.

```
240 NEXT I
```

LISTING CONTINUED BELOW

Calculating the co-ordinates

Each loop calculates the co-ordinates for the grid lines along one side of the grid. For example, lines 210-240 work out the co-ordinates for side 1. At line 220 the computer subtracts CX(1) from CX(2). This gives the number of X points along side 1. The first time through the loop it multiplies this figure by 1/N (N is the number of grid lines you chose). If, say, N is 5, this gives 1/5 of the length of side 1. Then it adds this figure to CX(1) and stores the answer in LX(1,1). The second time through the loop I=2 so it multiplies by 2/5 and stores the answer in LX(1,2). It does this for all the values for I from 1 to N to find all the X co-ordinates for the grid lines along side 1. Line 230 uses the same method to find the Y co-ordinates.

```
250 FOR I=1 TO N

260 LET LX(3,I)=CX(4)+(CX(3)-CX(4))*I/N

270 LET LY(3,I)=CY(4)+(CY(3)-CY(4))*I/N

280 NEXT I

290 FOR I=1 TO N

300 LET LX(2,I)=CX(2)+(CX(3)-CX(2))*I/N

310 LET LY(2,I)=CY(2)+(CY(3)-CY(2))*I/N

320 NEXT I
```

Loop to work out the co-ordinates for side 3. To store them in the same order as for side 1 (i.e. from left to right), the computer has to do the sum in the opposite order. It subtracts corner 4 from corner 3, then adds the result to corner 4.

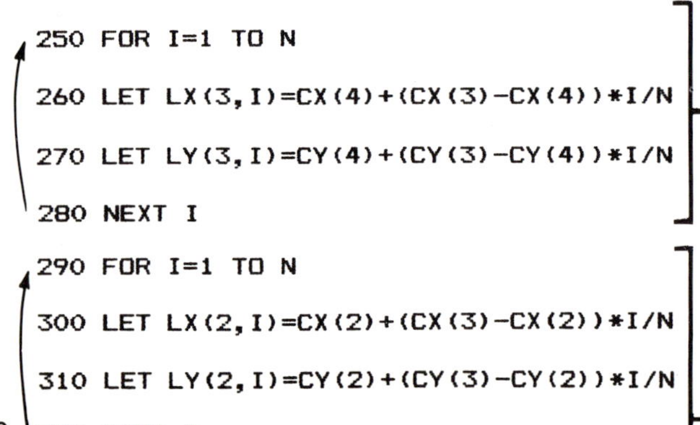

Loop to work out co-ordinates for side 2.

LISTING CONTINUED OPPOSITE

```
330 FOR I=1 TO N
340 LET LX(4,I)=CX(1)+(CX(4)-CX(1))*I/N
350 LET LY(4,I)=CY(1)+(CY(4)-CY(1))*I/N
360 NEXT I
```

Loop to work out co-ordinates for side 4.

```
400 REM DRAW GRID LINES
410 LET ROW=1: GOSUB 500
420 LET ROW=2: GOSUB 500
```

This line sets up a variable called ROW and gives it a value of 1. Then the computer goes to the subroutine at line 500. After the subroutine it returns to line 420 and changes ROW to 2, then goes to the subroutine again.

```
430 STOP
```

This stops the program after the subroutine has been carried out twice.

```
500 REM SUBROUTINE
510 FOR I=1 TO N
520 PLOT LX(ROW,I),LY(ROW,I)
530 DRAW LX(ROW+2,I),LY(ROW+2,I)
540 NEXT I
550 RETURN
```

ROW and I are the subscripts for LX and LY. They tell the computer which compartment to look in to find the X and Y co-ordinates for each grid line. ROW is the row number and I is the column. Row 1 holds the co-ordinates for side 1, row 2 for side 2, etc.

Back to line 420 the first time through the subroutine and 430 the second time.

Drawing the grid lines

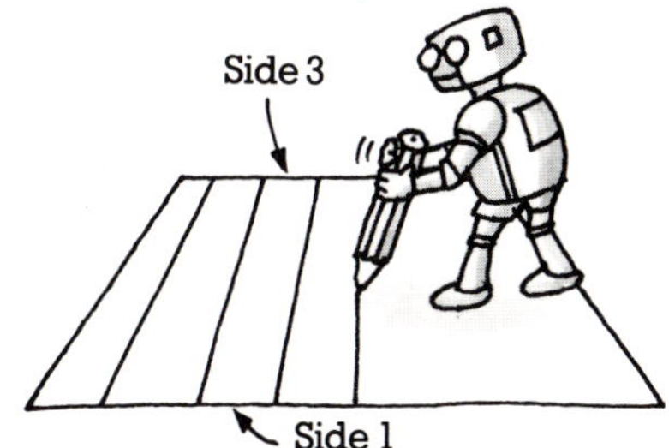

The first time through the subroutine ROW=1 so at line 520 the computer plots a point on side 1. At line 530 it adds 2 to ROW and so draws a line to side 3. The second time through the subroutine ROW=2 so it plots points on side 2 and draws lines to side 4.

Ideas for altering the program

1. To make different shaped grids, work out the co-ordinates for a shape you like on paper first. Remember that the first pair of figures in line 160 are the co-ordinates for corner 1, the second pair for corner 2, etc. If you make two corners the same you will get a triangle. See if you can make the sides cross over, as shown in the picture on the right on page 26.

2. You can use INPUT with a loop to make the computer ask you for the data. Replace lines 140-160 with the following lines:

```
140 FOR I=1 TO 4
150 PRINT "WHAT ARE THE CO-ORDINATES FOR CORNER ";I
155 INPUT CX(I),CY(I)
160 NEXT I
```

3. To make coloured grid lines, insert your computer's colour command before the GOSUB in lines 410 and 420. Remember to put a colon to separate the colour command from the GOSUB.

Programs for sorting data

Sometimes you need to sort data into alphabetical or numerical order, for instance, to arrange a magazine index, or analyze data collected about, say, the weather or wildlife sightings, or a local history survey. Short lists are quite easy to sort by hand, but with lots of data, a computer is far quicker and more accurate.

Special programs for sorting data are called "sorts". There are lots of different sort programs already written in BASIC – you may come across some in magazines. The different programs use different programming techniques and are useful for different tasks.

On the next few pages there are two different kinds of sort program. One is called a "bubble sort" (you can find out why below) and the other is a Shell sort (named after the person who wrote it). A bubble sort is one of the slowest kinds of sort and is only useful for small amounts of data. A Shell sort is much, much quicker. On page 35 there are some lines you can add to the programs to compare them and see how fast your computer is.

Bubble sort

In a bubble sort the computer starts at the beginning of the unsorted list and compares the first two items. If they are in the wrong order it swaps them around and then compares the next two items. It carries on like this all through the list so the larger numbers gradually "bubble" to the end of the list.

The following program is a bubble sort for numbers. Over the page there is another version of the program for sorting words.

```
100    REM    BUBBLE SORT FOR NUMBERS
110    INPUT "HOW MANY NUMBERS TO BE
SORTED? ";T
120    DIM N(T)
130    FOR I=1 TO T
140    PRINT "NUMBER ";I
150    INPUT N(I)
160    NEXT I
```

Sets up an array called N with T compartments. T is the total number of numbers you wish to sort.

Asks you for the numbers to be sorted and stores them in the array.

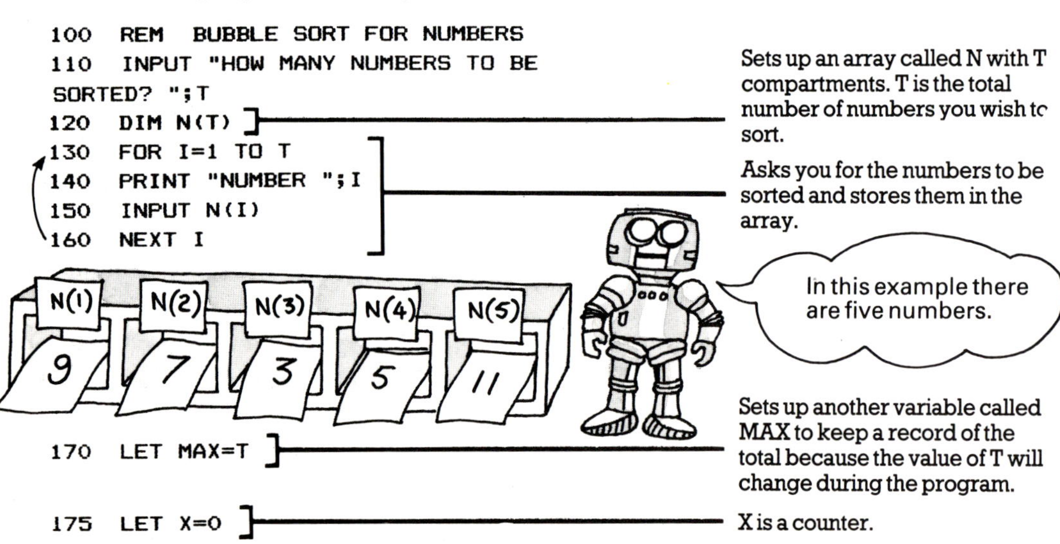


```
170    LET MAX=T
```

Sets up another variable called MAX to keep a record of the total because the value of T will change during the program.

```
175    LET X=0
```

X is a counter.

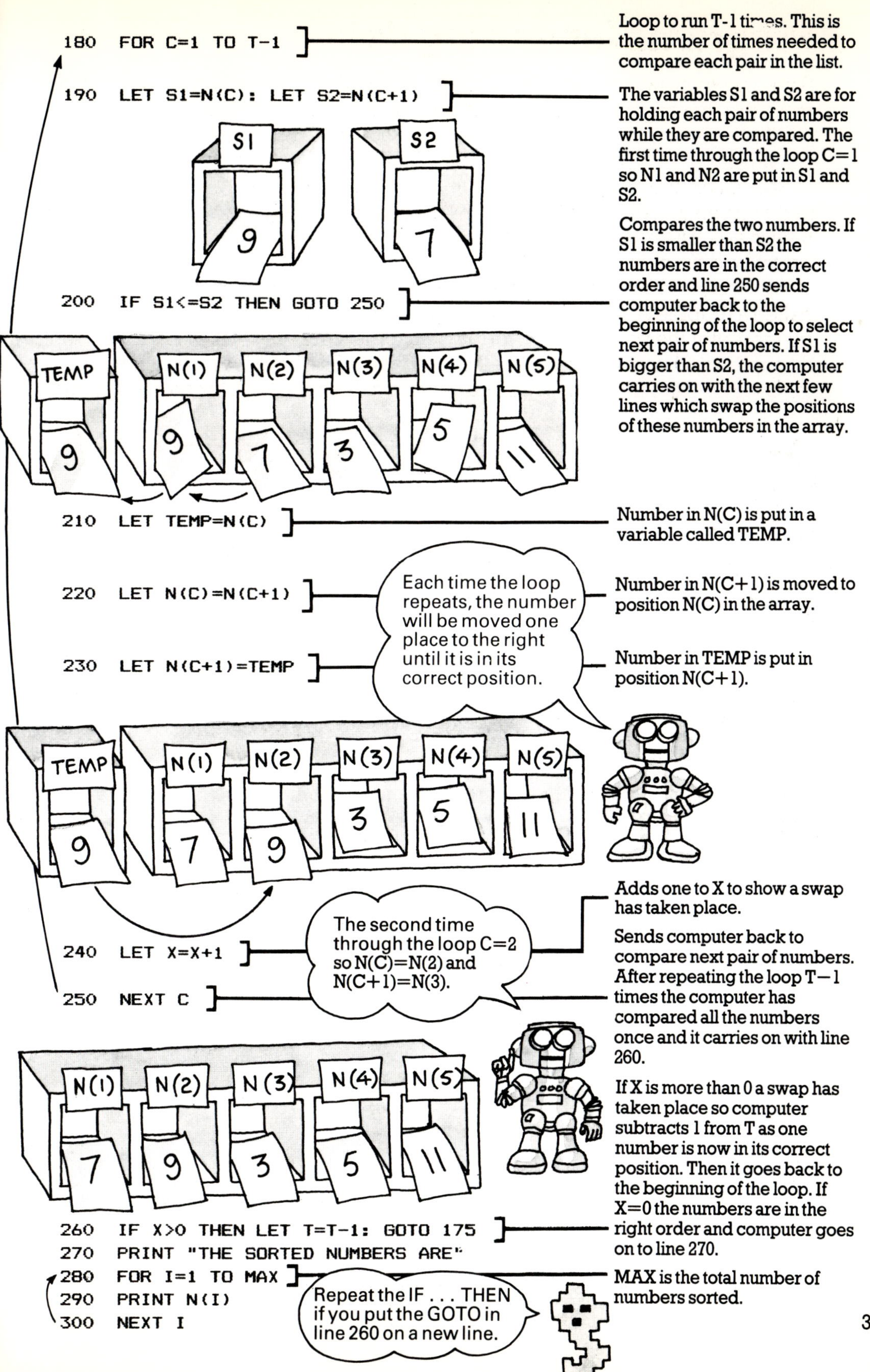

Loop to run T-1 times. This is the number of times needed to compare each pair in the list.

The variables S1 and S2 are for holding each pair of numbers while they are compared. The first time through the loop C=1 so N1 and N2 are put in S1 and S2.

Compares the two numbers. If S1 is smaller than S2 the numbers are in the correct order and line 250 sends computer back to the beginning of the loop to select next pair of numbers. If S1 is bigger than S2, the computer carries on with the next few lines which swap the positions of these numbers in the array.

Number in N(C) is put in a variable called TEMP.

Number in N(C+1) is moved to position N(C) in the array.

Number in TEMP is put in position N(C+1).

Adds one to X to show a swap has taken place.

Sends computer back to compare next pair of numbers. After repeating the loop T−1 times the computer has compared all the numbers once and it carries on with line 260.

If X is more than 0 a swap has taken place so computer subtracts 1 from T as one number is now in its correct position. Then it goes back to the beginning of the loop. If X=0 the numbers are in the right order and computer goes on to line 270.

MAX is the total number of numbers sorted.

Word bubble sort

The next program is a bubble sort for words. It is the same as the number bubble sort, except that the variables for holding the data (N, S1, S2, and TEMP) are string variables.*

The computer uses the same method to compare letters as it does numbers. Inside the computer letters and symbols are represented by numbers, so when you give the computer characters to compare, it compares their number codes. To compare two words, it checks the first letter of each word and if they are the same it compares the second and then the third and so on. You can put numbers as well as letters into string variables, so you can use the word bubble sort for data which contain words and numbers such as addresses or the entries for an index.

```
HOW MANY ITEMS TO BE SORTED? 4
ITEM 1
?DISK DRIVES 34 76 82 93
ITEM 2
?MACHINE CODE 55 72 85
ITEM 3
?SOUND 32
ITEM 4
?GRAPHICS 8 23 45
THE SORTED LIST IS
DISK DRIVES 34 76 82 93
GRAPHICS 8 23 45
MACHINE CODE 55 72 85
SOUND 32
```

```
HOW MANY ITEMS TO BE SORTED? 4
ITEM 1
?KELLER MARY 12 PANSY PLACE
ITEM 2
?SMITH JOHN 12 QUEEN STREET
ITEM 3
?JONES PETER 3356 WESTSIDE
ITEM 4
?FLAK JANE 34 RING ROAD
THE SORTED LIST IS
FLAK JANE 34 RING ROAD
JONES PETER 3356 WESTSIDE
KELLER MARY 12 PANSY PLACE
SMITH JOHN 12 QUEEN STREET
```

In this example the computer is sorting items for an index, and on the right, addresses. The items were typed in without commas as for most computers a comma is a separator, or "delimiter" between different items of information. If you want to use commas in strings, put the string in quotes.

The program

```
100   REM  BUBBLE SORT FOR WORDS
110   INPUT "HOW MANY ITEMS TO BE SORTED? ";T
120   DIM N$(T)
130   FOR I=1 TO T
140   PRINT "ITEM ";I
150   INPUT N$(I)
160   NEXT I
170   LET MAX=T
175   LET X=0
180   FOR C=1 TO T-1
190   LET S1$=N$(C): LET S2$=N$(C+1)
200   IF S1$<=S2$ THEN GOTO 250
210   LET TEMP$=N$(C)
220   LET N$(C)=N$(C+1)
230   LET N$(C+1)=TEMP$
240   LET X=X+1
250   NEXT C
260   IF X>0 THEN LET T=T-1: GOTO 175
270   PRINT "THE SORTED LIST IS"
280   FOR I=1 TO MAX
290   PRINT N$(I)
300   NEXT I
```

Sets up array called N$ with T compartments.

First two items are put in S1$ and S2$.

Compares S1$ and S2$.

Swaps the positions of the first two items in N$.

If X>0, subtracts 1 from total and goes back to beginning of loop to check through list again.

*For Sinclair (Timex) computers change line 120 to read DIM N$(T,N) where N is the length of the longest string you want to input.

Shell sort

If you want to sort lots of items the bubble sort is very slow. It can take almost a minute to sort fifty items on some computers. The next program is a Shell sort for numbers and it is about three times faster than a bubble sort.

In a Shell sort, the computer divides the list of items to be sorted in half, and checks all the items in one half against those in the other half. Then it divides the list in half again and does a lot more comparing and moving the larger numbers up the list using the same swapping technique as in the bubble sort.

The program

```
100   REM   SHELL SORT FOR NUMBERS
110   INPUT "HOW MANY NUMBERS TO
BE SORTED? ";T
120   DIM N(T)
130   FOR I=1 TO T
140   PRINT "NUMBER ";I
150   INPUT N(I)
160   NEXT I
170   LET C=T
180   LET C=INT(C/2)
190   IF C=0 THEN GOTO 330
200   LET D=T-C
210   LET E=1
220   LET F=E
230   LET G=F+C
```

These lines are just like the bubble sort. T is the total number of numbers to be sorted and lines 120 to 160 ask you for the numbers and store them in array N.

Sets variable C to equal the total number of items.

Divides C in half to give the number of items in the first half of the list. INT makes the computer discard any figures after the decimal point to make C a whole number.

The program repeatedly divides C in half, and when C=0 the computer goes to line 330 to print out the sorted list.

D is the number of items in the second part of the list.

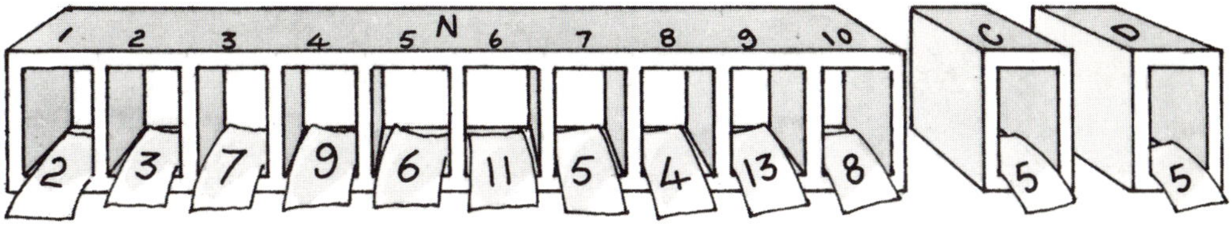

E is a counter.

The variables F and G are for setting the subscripts for N, the array where all the numbers are stored.

LISTING CONTINUED OVER THE PAGE

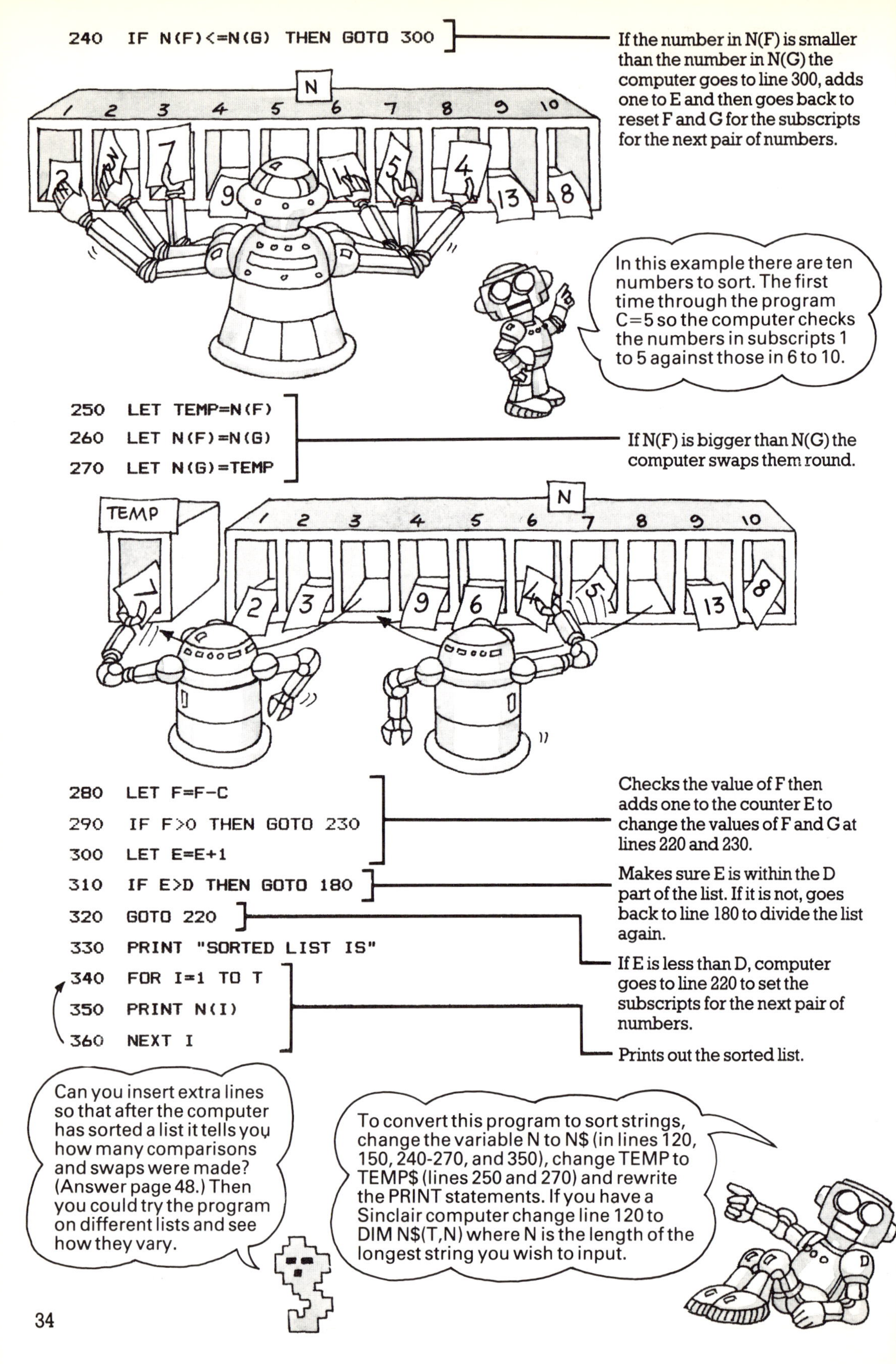

If the number in N(F) is smaller than the number in N(G) the computer goes to line 300, adds one to E and then goes back to reset F and G for the subscripts for the next pair of numbers.

If N(F) is bigger than N(G) the computer swaps them round.

Checks the value of F then adds one to the counter E to change the values of F and G at lines 220 and 230.

Makes sure E is within the D part of the list. If it is not, goes back to line 180 to divide the list again.

If E is less than D, computer goes to line 220 to set the subscripts for the next pair of numbers.

Prints out the sorted list.

How does it work?

To get a better idea of how the Shell sort works you could insert these extra lines. They print out the values of the variables so you can see which numbers the computer is comparing.

```
233  PRINT
235  PRINT  "F=";F;",G=";G          F and G are the subscripts of
237  PRINT  "COMPARE N(";F;") AND N(";G;")"   the numbers to be compared.
245  PRINT  "SWAP N(";F;") AND N(";G;")"    Tells you the subscripts of the
274  PRINT  "LIST=";                 numbers to be swapped.
275  FOR J=1 TO T
276  PRINT  N(J);" ";               Prints out the current
277  NEXT J                         arrangement of the list.
278  PRINT
279  INPUT"PRESS RETURN TO CONTINUE";Z$
```

Comparing sorts

If you tested the bubble and Shell sorts with just a few numbers, you may not have noticed how much faster the Shell sort is. To test the two sorts you could make them both generate a list of random numbers, and then time how long each program takes to sort them into order. The longer the list of numbers, the more the difference in time between the two sorts increases. Over the page there are some programs to plot graphs to show the difference between the two sorts.

Generating the numbers

```
140  LET N(I)=INT(RND(1)*200+1)
150  PRINT N(I)
165  INPUT "SET YOUR WATCH AND
PRESS RETURN TO START THE
SORT";Z$
```

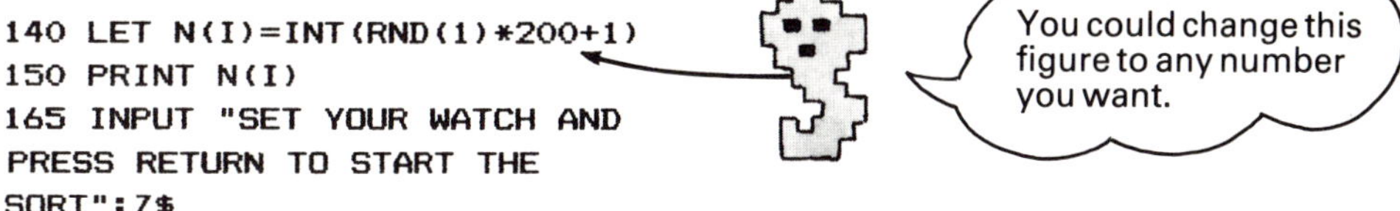

To make the programs generate their own list of numbers to sort you need to replace lines 140 and 150 in both programs and insert a new line 165 so you can control when the sort begins.

Line 140 generates random numbers between 1 and 200 and stores them in array N. Line 150 prints the numbers on the screen and line 165 makes the program wait until you press RETURN.

Running the test

To test each program you should run it several times, the first time to see how long it takes to sort, say, 10 numbers, then 20, 30, 40, etc. Different makes of computer will sort the lists at different speeds and some, like the ZX81 have a fast and slow mode. The following are the speeds on an Apple II.

Sorts test					
No. of numbers sorted	10	20	30	40	50
Bubble sort	2 sec	5 sec	11 sec	18 sec	29 sec
Shell sort	1 sec	2 sec	4 sec	6 sec	8 sec

Drawing graphs

Results from a computer are much easier to read and understand if you present
them in an interesting way, using graphics as well as words. Below there is a
program for a bar chart to show the difference between the bubble and Shell sorts.
On the opposite page you can find out how to convert the bar chart program to
make a line graph.

The programs are quite straightforward, and you could easily adapt them to
display different information. You could also improve them by adding the colour
commands for your computer to draw the graphs in different colours.

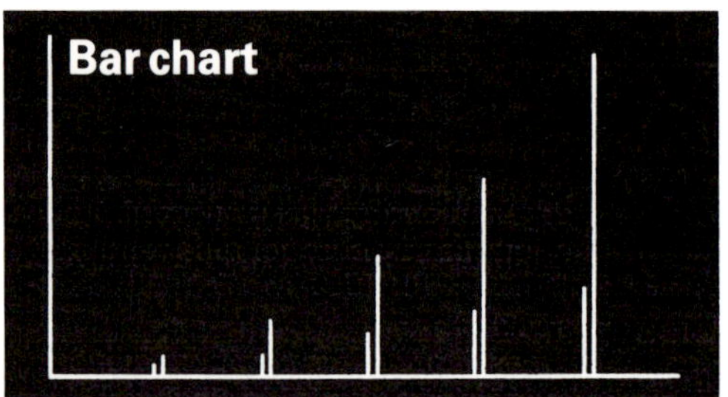

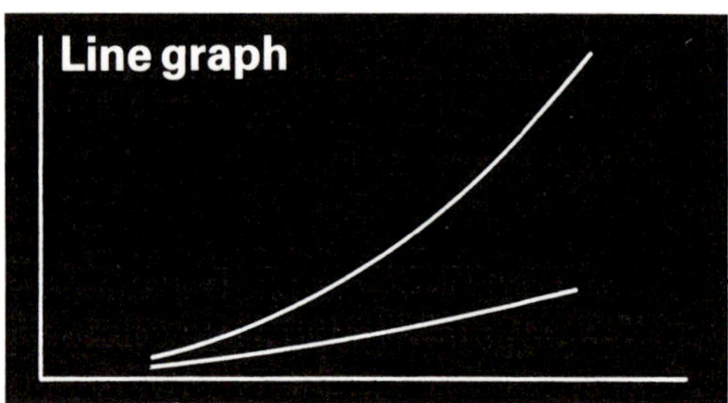

These are the screen displays for the two
graph programs. Both the graphs compare
the time taken by the two sorts to sort 10, 20,
30, 40 and 50 numbers. The time is shown up
the Y axis and the number of numbers

sorted is along the X axis. If your computer
can print text at pixel positions you can add
labels to make the graphs clearer. You can
find out how to do this for the BBC micro on
the opposite page.

Bar chart program

```
100 DIM B(5): DIM S(5)
110 LET N=0
120 FOR I=10 TO 50 STEP 10
130 LET N=N+1
140 PRINT FOR ";I;" NUMBERS"
150 INPUT "HOW MANY SECONDS DID THE
BUBBLE SORT TAKE? ";B(N)
160 INPUT "AND THE SHELL SORT? ";S(N)
170 NEXT I
180 INPUT "HOW MANY PLOT POSITIONS UP
YOUR SCREEN? ";H
190 INPUT "AND HOW MANY ACROSS? ";W
200 REM GIVE GRAPHICS MODE COMMAND
IF NECESSARY
```

Sets up arrays B and S to hold
data for bubble and Shell sorts.

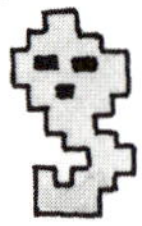

Loop to input data into the
arrays. N is a counter to set the
subscripts for the arrays.

Draws the axes 1 pixel in from
the edge of the screen. H and
W are the height and width of
your screen.

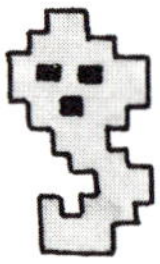

```
210 REM DRAW AXES
220 PLOT 1,H: DRAW 1,1: DRAW W,1
230 REM DRAW GRAPH
240 LET X=(W*0.75)/5
250 LET Y=(H*0.75)/B(5)
```

The figures for X and Y set the scale
for the graph along the X and Y axes.
X is three quarters of the width
divided by 5, the number of tests for
each sort. Y is three-quarters of the
height divided by the longest time,
i.e. B(5).

LISTING CONTINUED OPPOSITE

```
260 FOR I=1 TO 5
```

Can you change the bar chart program to make it draw thicker bars? (Answer page 48.)

Sets up loop to draw the bars. The loop variable I counts the tests and each time the loop repeats the computer draws a bar for each sort.

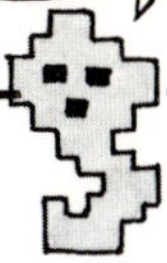

```
270 PLOT INT(I*X),1
```

Plots a point I⋆X along, and 1 pixel up. The first time through the loop I is 1 and X is the figure for the scale along the X axis.

```
280 DRAW INT(I*X),INT(B(I)*Y)
```

Draws a line to B(I)⋆Y. The first time through the loop I is 1 so B(I) is the time taken for 10 numbers and Y is the figure for the scale along the Y axis.

```
290 PLOT INT(I*X-4),1
```

For the BBC micro, change the figure −4 to −10.

Plots a point I⋆X−4 points along, i.e. 4 points to the left of the bar for the bubble sort.

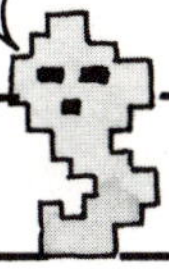

```
300 DRAW INT(I*X-4),INT(S(I)*Y)
```

Draws a line to S(I)⋆Y.

```
310 NEXT I
```

Goes back to the beginning of the loop to plot the next pair of bars.

If your computer can print text at pixel positions you can add lines to label the graphs. For instance, to do this on the BBC micro you would need the lines given below.

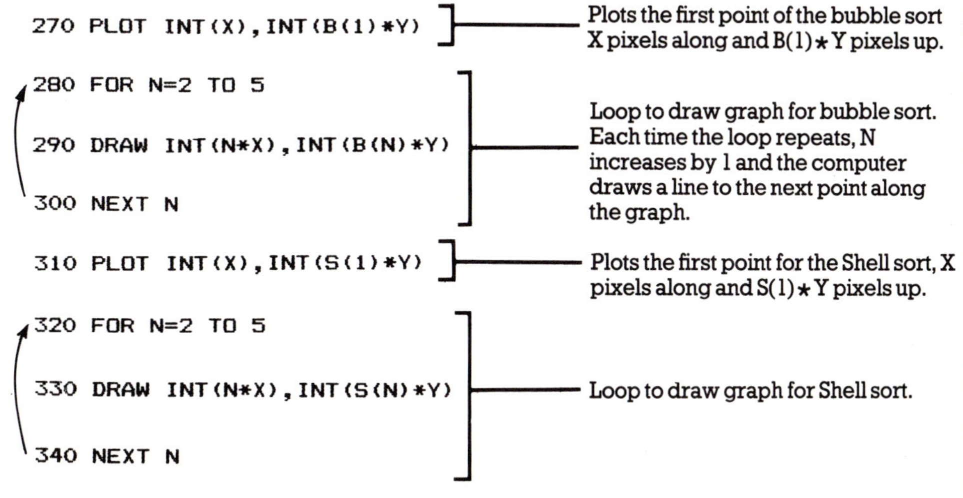

```
305 VDU 5:MOVE (I*X),INT(B(I)*Y)+50:PRINT "B"
308 VDU 5:MOVE (I*X)-70,INT(S(I)*Y)+50:PRINT "S"
```

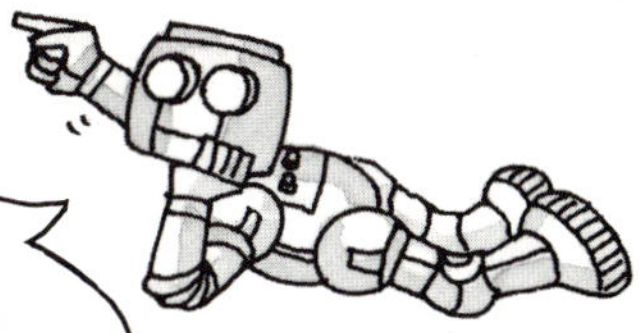

Line graph program

For a line graph you need to plot the first point of the graph, then draw a line to each point along the graph. To do this you need separate loops for each sort. To convert the bar chart program to make a line graph replace lines 270 onwards with the following lines:

```
270 PLOT INT(X),INT(B(1)*Y)
```

Plots the first point of the bubble sort X pixels along and B(1)⋆Y pixels up.

```
280 FOR N=2 TO 5
290 DRAW INT(N*X),INT(B(N)*Y)
300 NEXT N
```

Loop to draw graph for bubble sort. Each time the loop repeats, N increases by 1 and the computer draws a line to the next point along the graph.

```
310 PLOT INT(X),INT(S(1)*Y)
```

Plots the first point for the Shell sort, X pixels along and S(1)⋆Y pixels up.

```
320 FOR N=2 TO 5
330 DRAW INT(N*X),INT(S(N)*Y)
340 NEXT N
```

Loop to draw graph for Shell sort.

More string handling

The program on the next few pages makes the computer appear to have a conversation with you. Of course, the computer is only as clever as the program you give it and all the words and phrases for its replies are held in string arrays in the program.*

The program's main task is to make the computer choose the right words to reply to you. It contains some BASIC string handling routines which make its replies seem almost "intelligent" at times. The success of such a program lies not only in the structure of the program but also in the words and phrases you build in to it. You could try changing the computer's vocabulary to make it "talk" about different subjects, or make its replies more friendly . . . or grumpy.

Sample runs

```
HELLO, WHAT'S YOUR NAME? JUDY
TALK TO ME, JUDY
?HELLO COMPUTER
WHAT DO YOU THINK ABOUT THE NEWS?
?WHAT NEWS?
THAT'S A GOOD QUESTION
?AREN'T YOU GOING TO TELL ME?
LISTEN JUDY, I THINK YOU ARE JUST
AS FRIENDLY AS THE OTHER PEOPLE I
HAVE TALKED TO
?THANKS
DON'T MENTION IT
```

```
?WHAT DO YOU WANT TO TALK ABOUT?
TELL ME ABOUT THE WEATHER, JUDY
?IT'S RAINING
WHAT MAKES YOU SO SURE
?I CAN SEE IT
I'VE HEARD THAT YOU ARE SOME KIND
OF WITTY GENIUS JUDY
?WHO TOLD YOU?
IT DOESN'T MATTER
?WHY WON'T YOU ANSWER MY QUESTIONS?
MY DEAR FRIEND JUDY, YOU DON'T
THINK ALL HUMANS ARE RUDE DO YOU?
```

How it works

There are two different methods in the program for producing the computer's replies. One is a "phrase checking" routine and the other is a random sentence generator.

The phrase checking routine has a list of frequently used words and phrases stored in an array called Q$. For each word or phrase there is a suitable reply stored in M$. When you type something in the computer checks to see if you have used any of the Q$ phrases, and if you have, it uses the corresponding reply from M$.

*To convert the program for Sinclair (Timex) computers see page 47.

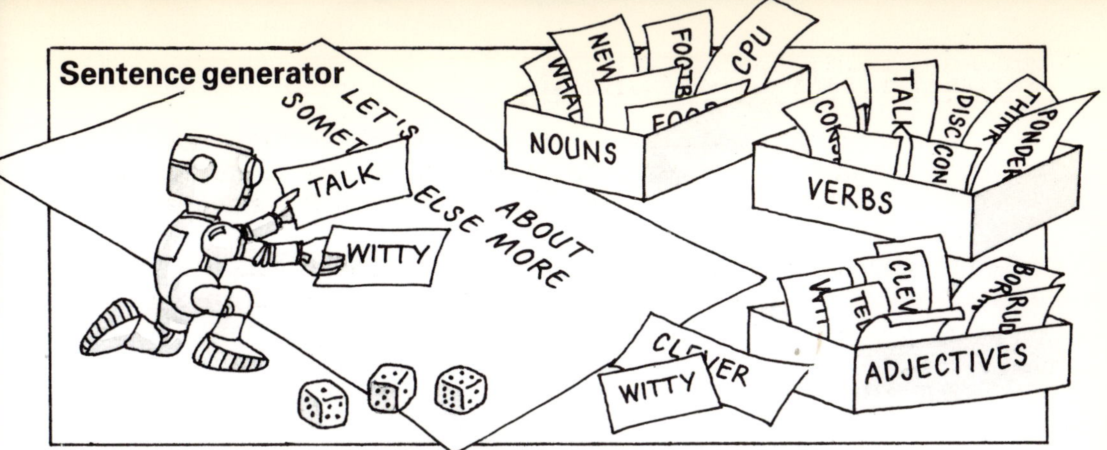

The random sentence generator consists of half-formed sentences which the computer completes with verbs, nouns and adjectives chosen at random. All the words are stored in arrays in the computer's memory and they have been specially chosen to make sense in the sentences.

What the variables are for

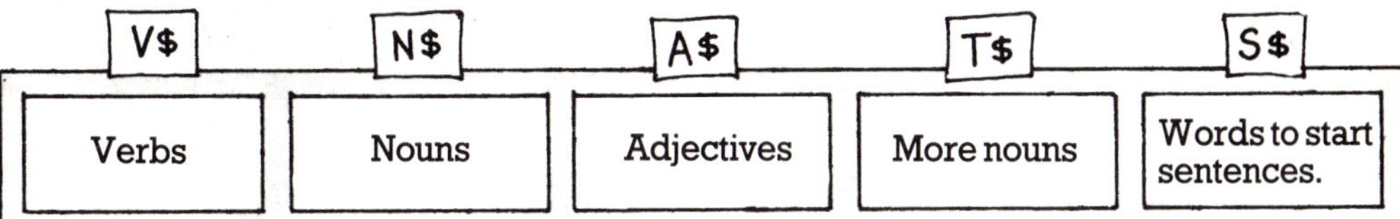

These are the arrays to hold the words for the random sentences.

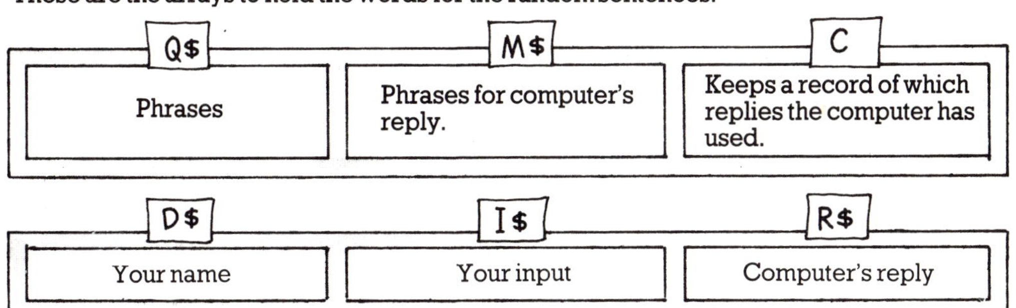

The program

```
100   CLS
110   DIM V$(10),N$(10),A$(10)
120   DIM T$(10),S$(10)
130   DIM M$(30),Q$(30),C(30)
140   REM READ IN DATA
150   GOSUB 1000
200   REM PERSON'S INPUT
210   INPUT "HELLO, WHAT'S YOUR NAME? ";D$
220   PRINT
230   PRINT "TALK TO ME, ";D$
240   INPUT I$
250   IF I$="" THEN GOTO 220
260   IF I$="BYE" THEN  GOTO 910
```

Sets up the arrays to hold the words and phrases. (N.B. On some computers you do not need to dimension arrays of less than ten elements.)

Goes to a subroutine to read all the words and phrases into the arrays.

Your reply to computer is held in I$.

Safeguard in case user just presses RETURN and I$ is empty.

If you type BYE the computer goes to line 910 to ask if you want to stop running the program.

LISTING CONTINUED OVER THE PAGE.

300 REM COMPUTER'S RESPONSE	
310 LET REPLY=INT(RND(1)*8+1)	The random number in the variable REPLY decides which method the computer will use for its response. If REPLY is less than 6 it uses the phrase checking routine which starts at line 490.
320 . IF REPLY<6 THEN GOTO 490	
330 GOTO 600	If REPLY is 6 or above it goes to the sentence generator at line 600.
340 PRINT	
350 PRINT R$	After working out its reply the computer stores it in R$, then prints it on the screen at line 350.
360 PRINT	
400 REM CHECK HOW MANY RESPONSES HAVE BEEN USED	

LISTING CONTINUED BELOW

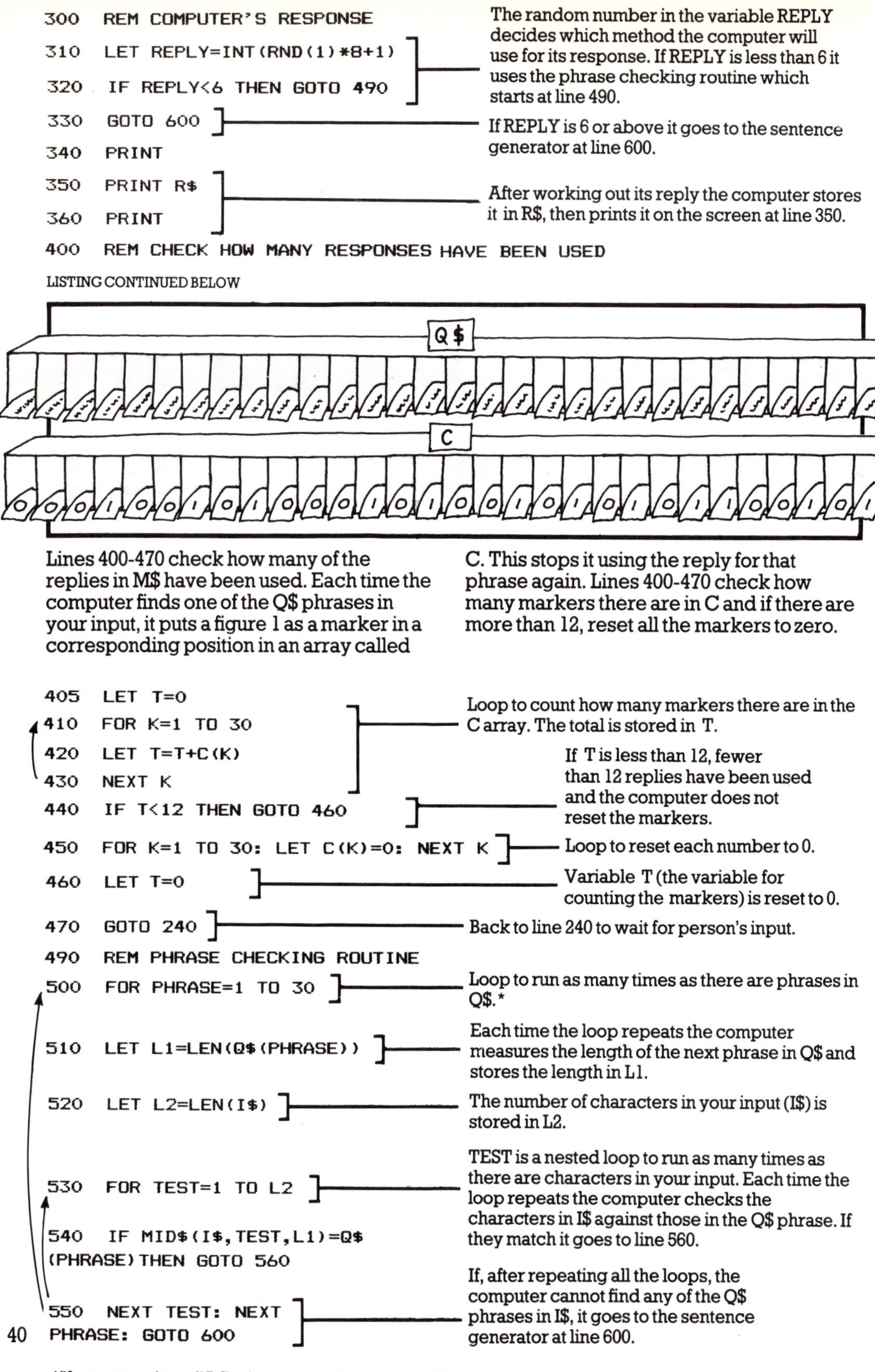

Lines 400-470 check how many of the replies in M$ have been used. Each time the computer finds one of the Q$ phrases in your input, it puts a figure 1 as a marker in a corresponding position in an array called C. This stops it using the reply for that phrase again. Lines 400-470 check how many markers there are in C and if there are more than 12, reset all the markers to zero.

405 LET T=0	
410 FOR K=1 TO 30	Loop to count how many markers there are in the C array. The total is stored in T.
420 LET T=T+C(K)	
430 NEXT K	
440 IF T<12 THEN GOTO 460	If T is less than 12, fewer than 12 replies have been used and the computer does not reset the markers.
450 FOR K=1 TO 30: LET C(K)=0: NEXT K	Loop to reset each number to 0.
460 LET T=0	Variable T (the variable for counting the markers) is reset to 0.
470 GOTO 240	Back to line 240 to wait for person's input.
490 REM PHRASE CHECKING ROUTINE	
500 FOR PHRASE=1 TO 30	Loop to run as many times as there are phrases in Q$.*
510 LET L1=LEN(Q$(PHRASE))	Each time the loop repeats the computer measures the length of the next phrase in Q$ and stores the length in L1.
520 LET L2=LEN(I$)	The number of characters in your input (I$) is stored in L2.
530 FOR TEST=1 TO L2	TEST is a nested loop to run as many times as there are characters in your input. Each time the loop repeats the computer checks the characters in I$ against those in the Q$ phrase. If they match it goes to line 560.
540 IF MID$(I$,TEST,L1)=Q$(PHRASE) THEN GOTO 560	
550 NEXT TEST: NEXT PHRASE: GOTO 600	If, after repeating all the loops, the computer cannot find any of the Q$ phrases in I$, it goes to the sentence generator at line 600.

40

*If you are using a BBC micro, see note on page 46.

```
560   IF C(PHRASE) >0 THEN GOTO 550
570   LET C(PHRASE)=C(PHRASE)+1
580   LET R$=M$(PHRASE)
590   GOTO 340
```

If it finds a matching phrase it jumps out of the loop and comes to line 560. Then it checks the marker in C array which corresponds to the phrase. If the marker is not 0 it goes back to the loops to see if there is another matching phrase in I$. If the marker is 0 it changes it to 1 at line 570. Then at line 580 it looks up the corresponding phrase in M$ and puts it in R$ ready to be printed out at line 350.

LISTING CONTINUED BELOW

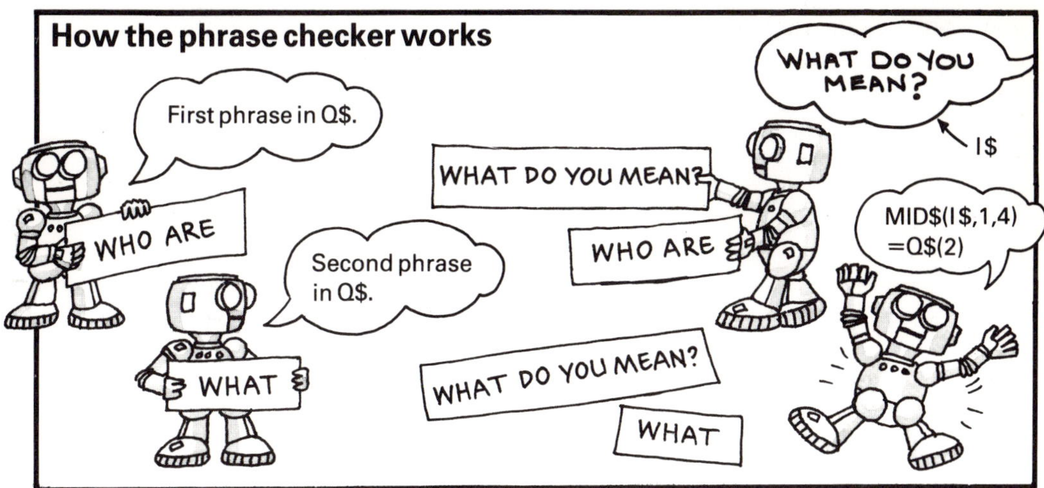

How the phrase checker works

The first time through the phrase checking routine PHRASE=1 so the computer examines the first phrase in Q$. The first time through the TEST loop, TEST=1 so the computer compares the Q$ phrase with characters 1 to 7 (the length of Q$) of I$. If they are not equal it repeats the TEST loop. This time TEST=2 so it compares characters 2 to 8, and so on. If the characters in I$ do not equal Q$ the computer goes back to the beginning of the PHRASE loop to select the next phrase from Q$.

```
600   REM SENTENCE GENERATOR
610   LET E=INT(RND(1)*10+1)
620   LET F=INT(RND(1)*10+1)
630   LET G=INT(RND(1)*10+1)
640   LET H=INT(RND(1)*10+1)
650   LET L=INT(RND(1)*10+1)
660   ON E GOTO 700,720,740,760,
      780,800,830,850,870,890
700   LET R$="WHAT DO YOU THINK
ABOUT "+N$(H)+"?"
710   GOTO 340
720   LET R$=S$(L)+" "+D$+" YOU DON'T
THINK ALL HUMANS ARE "+A$(G)+" DO YOU?"
730   GOTO 340
740   LET R$="I'VE HEARD THAT YOU ARE
SOME KIND OF "+A$(G)+" "+T$(H)+" "+D$
750   GOTO 340
760   LET R$=S$(L)+" "+D$+" , I THINK YOU ARE
JUST AS "+A$(G)
```

Random numbers to choose which words and sentence to use. The number for E decides which sentence the computer will use. F is for verbs, G is for adjectives, H is for nouns and L is for sentence starters.

The number in E tells the computer which line number to go to. If E=1 it goes to the first number in the list. If E=2 it goes to the second, etc. For more about the BASIC word ON, see page 20.

Lines 700-900 contain ten partly formed sentences which the computer fills in with the words from N$, V$, etc. To make the computer add strings like this you use a + sign. You have to be careful to put spaces in quotes, too, so that the sentences are properly spaced. The computer puts the complete sentence in R$ and then goes back to line 340 to print it out.

41

LISTING CONTINUED OVER THE PAGE

```
765   LET R$=R$+" AS THE OTHER PEOPLE I'VE TALKED TO"
770   GOTO 340
780   LET R$="I AM FEELING "+A$(G)+" NOW"
790   GOTO 340
800   PRINT: PRINT "SSSHHHH.....I AM THINKING ...."
810   LET R$="LETS "+V$(F)+" "+N$(H)+" I THINK "+N$(H)+" IS "+A$(G)
820   GOTO 340
830   LET R$="TELL ME ABOUT "+N$(H)+", "+D$
840   GOTO 340
850   LET R$="DO YOU THINK I AM "+A$(G)+", "+D$+"?"
860   GOTO 340
870   LET R$="LETS "+V$(F)+" SOMETHING ELSE MORE "+A$(G)
880   GOTO 340
890   LET R$="GUESS WHAT I AM THINKING "+D$
900   GOTO 340
910   REM BYE ROUTINE
920   PRINT "HAD ENOUGH ALREADY?"
930   PRINT "ISN'T THERE ANYONE HERE I CAN TALK TO ...?"
940   INPUT Z$: IF Z$="YES" GOTO 210
950   PRINT: PRINT "BYE THEN"
960   END
1000   REM PHRASES FOR PHRASE CHECKING ROUTINE
1010   FOR I=1 TO 30: READ Q$(I): NEXT I
1020   DATA WHO ARE, WHAT, ?, MEAN, WHY, YOUR
1030   DATA "ME ","I "," IT ",TALK, " NO "
1040   DATA ?," ARE "," MY ","YES",YOU,?
1050   DATA THINK, CLEVER, RUDE, THANK," OFF"
1060   DATA THEY,?, UNDERS," NOT "," IS "
1070   DATA TO, ?, KNOW
1100   REM COMPUTER'S REPLIES TO PHRASES IN Q$
1110   FOR I=1 TO 30: READ M$(I): NEXT I
1120   DATA I AM ONLY A COMPUTER
1130   DATA IT DOESN'T MATTER, THAT'S A
GOOD QUESTION
1140   DATA I DON'T KNOW, "WELL, WHY NOT?"
1150   DATA HOW DO YOU MEAN, "WHO ARE YOU?"
1160   DATA OH, WHAT DOES 'IT' MEAN
1170   DATA DO YOU WANT ME TO SHUT UP,
YOU'RE BEING A BIT NEGATIVE
1180   DATA YOU TELL ME, HOW DO YOU MEAN
1190   DATA MY-MY-MY, SO YOU AGREE
1200   DATA DON'T YOU LIKE ME
1210   DATA WHY, MAKE UP YOUR MIND, THANKS
1220   DATA YOU'VE SEEN NOTHING YET
1230   DATA DON'T MENTION IT
1240   DATA AND YOU, I DON'T CARE, WHAT A
STUPID QUESTION
1250   DATA YOU'VE GOT A LOW I.Q., RUBBISH
1260   DATA WHAT MAKES YOU SO SURE, GO AWAY
1270   DATA GET LOST, KNOWLEDGE IS A PROBLEM FOR ME
1300   REM READ IN NOUNS
1310   FOR I=1 TO 10: READ N$(I): NEXT I
1320   DATA FOOTBALL, BALLROOM DANCING
1340   DATA THE WEATHER, THE NEWS
1350   DATA MY CPU, FISHING
1360   DATA THE BLUE WHALE, EVOLUTION
1370   DATA GEOGRAPHY, FOOD
```


If your reply to computer is BYE, line 260 sends computer here.

These lines contain the phrases which the computer looks for in your input. Be careful to type them in exactly as they are here as the spaces inside the quotes are part of the data.

These are the computer's replies for each of the phrases in Q$. The replies are in the same order as the phrases. For example, the fifth item in M$ is the reply for the fifth phrase in Q$.

These are the nouns to put in the random sentences.

```
1400    REM READ IN VERBS
1410    FOR I=1 TO 10: READ V$(I): NEXT I
1420    DATA THINK ABOUT, TALK ABOUT
1430    DATA DISCUSS, CONTEMPLATE
1440    DATA REFLECT ON, MEDITATE ON
1450    DATA COGITATE, PONDER
1460    DATA CEREBRATE, CONSIDER
1500    REM READ IN ADJECTIVES
1510    FOR I=1 TO 10: READ A$(I): NEXT I
1520    DATA STUPID, CLEVER
1530    DATA INTELLIGENT, WISE
1540    DATA WITTY, FRIENDLY
1550    DATA TEDIOUS, TIRESOME
1560    DATA RUDE, NEUROTIC
1600    REM READ IN SENTENCE STARTERS AND
OTHER NOUNS, IN PAIRS
1610    FOR I=1 TO 10: READ S$(I),T$(I): NEXT I
1620    DATA GOOD HEAVENS, BORE
1630    DATA "WELL, ", TOAD
1640    DATA LET'S SEE, WHIZZ KID
1650    DATA LISTEN, GENIUS
1660    DATA LOOK, DUMBO
1670    DATA "UMMM...",MORON
1680    DATA NOW, PARASITE
1690    DATA REALLY, PRODIGY
1700    DATA OH NO, MONSTER
1710    DATA MY DEAR FRIEND, COMPUTER-FREAK
1720    RETURN
```

These are the verbs for the random sentences.

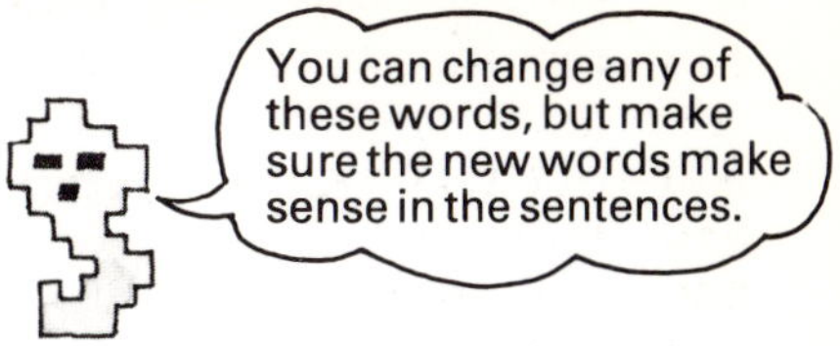

You can change any of these words, but make sure the new words make sense in the sentences.

These are the adjectives.

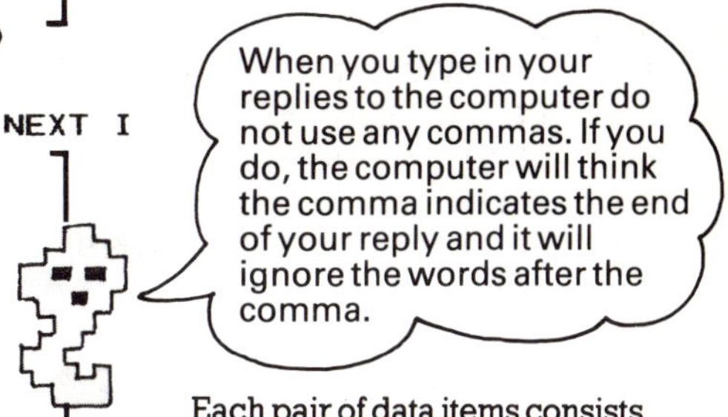

When you type in your replies to the computer do not use any commas. If you do, the computer will think the comma indicates the end of your reply and it will ignore the words after the comma.

Each pair of data items consists of a word to start a sentence and a noun. They are read in pairs to save space.

Ideas for changing the program

1.   The easiest way to alter the program is to change the words and sentences. It is best to check each word in each sentence to make sure it makes sense. At the moment, all the nouns in N$ are singular. If you use plural nouns, you will need to change the verbs. You could add extra words if you like. If you do, you will need to change the size of the arrays, the loops to read in the data and the random numbers in lines 610-650.

2.   You could also try changing the words in Q$ to make the computer spot different phrases. You will need to think up suitable replies for each new phrase and put the replies in the correct positions in M$.

3.   To make the computer use the random sentence generator more often, change the figure 6 in line 320 to a lower number. You can also change the frequency with which the computer resets the response markers in array C. To do this, change the figure 12 in line 440.

Daydream mode

You can make the computer "talk" to itself by adding the following lines to the program:

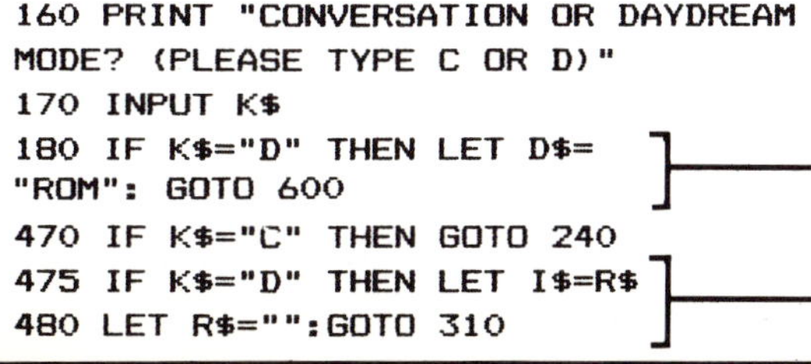


```
160 PRINT "CONVERSATION OR DAYDREAM
MODE? (PLEASE TYPE C OR D)"
170 INPUT K$
180 IF K$="D" THEN LET D$=
"ROM": GOTO 600
470 IF K$="C" THEN GOTO 240
475 IF K$="D" THEN LET I$=R$
480 LET R$="":GOTO 310
```

D$ was the variable to hold your name. In daydream mode the computer uses the word ROM as a name for itself, then goes to line 600 to generate a random sentence.

The computer's response, R$, becomes the new input, I$. Then the computer goes back to line 310 to choose its method of reply.

Answering back routine

On these two pages there is another routine you could add to the conversation program. It makes the computer answer you back using your own words. The conversions for Sinclair computers are given at the bottom of the opposite page.

The answering back routine works in a similar way to the phrase checking routine. There are two data arrays, U$ and W$. U$ contains phrases you might use in your input and W$ contains the computer's replies. If you use one of the U$ phrases, the answering back routine replaces it with the corresponding W$ phrase then adds the rest of your sentence.

`135   DIM U$(9),W$(9)` `138   DIM Z$(5)`	Sets up the arrays for U$ and W$ and another array called Z$ to hold the computer's replies.
`155   GOSUB 2200`	Goes to the subroutine to read in the data.
`325   IF REPLY=7 THEN GOTO 2000`	Tells the computer when to use the answering back routine.
`2000 REM ANSWERING BACK ROUTINE`	
`2010   LET Z=0`	Z is a counter.
`2020   LET P=LEN(I$)`	i.e. the number of characters in your input.
`2030   FOR A=1 TO P`	Loop to run as many times as there are characters in your input. *
`2040   FOR B=1 TO 9`	Loop to run as many times as there are characters in the longest item in W$.
`2050   LET L=LEN(U$(B))`	Each time B loop repeats, length of the next item in U$ is put in L.
`2060   IF  MID$(I$,A,L)=U$(B)  THEN GOTO 2140`	Compares characters A to L of your input with the phrase with the subscript of the value of B in U$ (B is set by loop). If phrases match, computer goes to line 2140.
`2070   NEXT B: NEXT A`	Each time B loop repeats computer checks next phrase in U$. When the A loop repeats it takes the next sequence of characters in I$.
`2080   IF Z$(1)="" THEN GOTO 600`	Back to random sentence generator if no phrases match.

*If you are using a BBC micro, see note on page 46.

```
2090    FOR J=1 TO Z
2100    PRINT Z$(J);
2110    LET Z$(J)=""
2120    NEXT J
2130    LET R$=I$: GOTO 350
2140    LET Z=Z+1

2150    IF A>1 THEN LET Z$(Z)=LEFT$
(I$,A-1)+" "+W$(B)+" "

2160    IF A<2 THEN LET Z$(Z)=W$(B)+" "

2170    LET I$=MID$(I$,A+L,P)

2180    GOTO 2020
2200    REM DATA FOR ANSWERING BACK ROUTINE
2210    FOR I=1 TO 9
2220    READ U$(I),W$(I)
2230    NEXT I
2240    DATA I AM, YOU ARE, YOU ARE, I AM
2250    DATA "I ", YOU, " ME", YOU
2260    DATA " MY ", "YOUR ", "YOURS ", MINE
2270    DATA " YOUR ", " MY ", " MINE", YOURS
2280    DATA YOU, COMPUTERS
2290    RETURN
```

- Prints out all the replies in Z$.
- Puts any remaining part of your sentence in R$ then goes back to line 350 to print it out.
- Z keeps count of replies in Z$.
- Variable A is set by loop at line 2030 and it is the number of the first character of the phrase in I$ which matches the U$ phrase. If A>1 line 2150 puts the characters to the left of the phrase in Z$, then adds the reply from W$.
- If A<2 then the matching phrase is at the beginning of I$ so computer puts just its reply in Z$.
- Puts the rest of your sentence into Z$ then goes back to the loops to see if there is another matching phrase.
- This is the data for U$ and W$.

Answering back routine for Sinclair computers

Insert the following lines for both the Spectrum and the ZX81. For the ZX81, though, you will have to use the method given on page 47 for the Conversation program to input the data. Put the ZX81's input loop between lines 1000 and 1720 and the DIM statements before line 1000.

```
135     DIM U$(9,7)
136     DIM W$(9,9)
137     DIM Z$(5,20)
2042    LET P$=""
2044    FOR I=1 TO LEN(U$(B))
2046    IF U$(B)(I TO I)<>"*" THEN LET P$=P$+U$(B)(I TO I)
2048    NEXT I
2050    LET L=LEN(P$)
2055    IF L+A-1>P THEN GOTO 2070
2060    IF I$(A TO A+L-1)=P$ THEN GOTO 2140
2080    IF Z=0 THEN GOTO 600
2150    IF A>1 THEN LET Z$(Z)=I$(TO A-1)+" "+W$(B)+" "
2160    IF A<2 THEN LET Z$(Z)=W$(B)+" "
2170    LET I$=I$(A+L TO)
2240    DATA "I AM***","YOU ARE","YOU ARE","I AM"
2250    DATA "I *****","YOU"," ME****","YOU"
2260    DATA " MY ***","YOUR","YOURS *","MINE"
2270    DATA " YOUR *", "MY"," MINE**", "YOURS"
2280    DATA "YOU ***","COMPUTERS"
2290    RETURN
```

- Puts a U$ phrase in P$ using the *s to find the end of the phrase.
- If P$ is longer than I$ phrase, goes back to select next phrase.
- If I$ phrase=P$ phrase goes to 2140.
- If no phrases match, goes to random sentence generator.
- If A>1 puts characters at beginning of I$ into Z$ and adds W$ phrase. If A<2 just puts W$ phrase in Z$.
- The spaces are an important part of the data, so you have to pad out the strings with *s.

Converting the programs

These two pages show you how to convert the programs to run on the ZX81 and Spectrum and how to convert the graphics programs to run on computers which draw lines relative to the last point plotted. As well as inserting the lines given here, you also have to make the other changes necessary for your computer, e.g. use your computer's graphics commands and RND instruction and change variable names if necessary.

Sinclair (Timex) computers Word Spotting Game

Change CHECK$ to C$ and replace lines 170 and 200 with the following:

```
170 LET L$=W$(R TO R)
200 LET C$=C$(2 TO)+L$
```

Spectrum (Timex 2000) Database

```
10 DIM T$(10,14):DIM Y(12):
15 DIM M(10,12)
120 ⎤
417 ⎬— Same as ZX81
425 ⎦
```

Remember to put quotes round each item in the DATA lines.

ZX81 (Timex 1000) Database

```
10 DIM T$(10,14)
12 DIM Y(12)
14 DIM M$(10,12)
```
Second subscript is the length of the longest string.

```
120 GOSUB 100+100*C
```
Uses C to calculate line number.

```
417 LET L=LEN(Z$)
425 IF Z$=T$(I)(1 TO L) THEN GOTO 440
```
Tells the computer which characters to check.

```
455 IF VAL(M$(I,J))=1 THEN PRINT "WON
THE WORLD CUP IN ";Y(J)
460 IF VAL(M$(I,J))=2 THEN PRINT "WAS A
FINALIST IN ";Y(J)
555 IF VAL(M$(J,I)=1 THEN PRINT T$(J);" WON
THE CUP"
```
The matrix data is stored in a string array, so you need VAL to tell computer to take numeric value.

```
2170 IF C>0 AND C<6 THEN GOTO 2180
2175 PRINT "PLEASE ENTER A FIGURE
BETWEEN 1 AND 5"
2176 GOTO 2150
```

Instead of inputting all the years you can make the computer calculate them with the following lines:

```
1000 FOR I=1 TO 3
1010 LET Y(I)=1926+I*4
1020 NEXT I
1030 FOR I=0 TO 8
1040 LET Y(I+4)=1950+4*I
1050 NEXT I
```

Replace lines 1100 to 1120 with ten LET statements, e.g.

```
1100 LET T$(1)="URUGUAY"
1110 LET T$(2)="ARGENTINA"
```

Replace lines 1200-1310 with ten more LET statements, e.g.

```
1200 LET M$(1)="100100000000"
1210 LET M$(2)="200000000010"
```

Add a new line:

```
1310 RETURN
```

BBC Database and Conversation program

Both these programs use loops to check through data, then jump out of the loops when the data item has been found. The BBC micro will only let you do this ten times after which you will get the error message "TOO MANY FORS". To avoid this, change the loops to variable counters with IF . . . THEN statements. For example, use the following lines in the Database:

```
420 LET I=0
422 LET I=I+1
430 IF I<10 GOTO 422
520 LET I=0
522 LET I=I+1
530 IF I<12 GOTO 522
```

You will need to do the same for lines 500-550 of the Conversation program and lines 2030-2070 of the answering back routine.

```
Instant Graphics and drawing graphs
```

Instant Graphics and drawing graphs

For computers (e.g. Spectrum and Oric) which draw lines to a point X,Y measured from the previous point plotted and not from the corner of the screen replace the following lines in the Instant Graphics and graphs programs. (You will need to replace DRAW and PLOT with your computer's graphics commands.)

Instant Graphics

```
175   DRAW CX(1)-CX(4),CY(1)-CY(4)
180   FOR I=2 TO 4
185   DRAW CX(I)-CX(I-1),CY(I)-CY(I-1)
530   DRAW LX(ROW+2,I)-LX(ROW,I),
LY(ROW+2,I)-LY(ROW,I)
```

To find the co-ordinates for the end of the lines the computer subtracts the co-ordinates of the last point plotted.

Bar Chart

```
220   PLOT 1,H:DRAW 0,-H+1:DRAW W,0
300   DRAW 0, INT(B(I)*Y)
320   DRAW 0, INT(S(I)*Y)
```

Line Graph

```
290   DRAW X, INT((B(N)-B(N-1))*Y)
330   DRAW X, INT((S(N)-S(N-1))*Y)
```

Spectrum (Timex 2000) Conversation program

Make the following changes for the Spectrum:

```
110   DIM V$(10,11):DIM N$(10,16):DIM A$(10,11)
120   DIM T$(10,14):DIM S$(10,14)
130   DIM M$(30,29):DIM Q$(30,7) DIM C(30)
245   PRINT I$
500   FOR Q=1 TO 30                           ── Use Q instead of PHRASE.
510   LET P$=""
512   FOR I=1 TO LEN (Q$(Q))
514    IF Q$(Q)(I TO I)<>" " THEN             ── Puts Q$ phrase in P$.
LET P$=P$+Q$(Q)(I TO I)
516   NEXT I
530   FOR T=1 TO L2-LEN(P$)+1
540    IF I$(T TO T+LEN(P$)-1)=P$ THEN        ── Checks to see if I$=P$.
GOTO 560
550   NEXT T:NEXT Q: GOTO 600
560
570  ─Change variable PHRASE to Q.
580
660   GOTO ((E<7)*(680+E*20))+((E>6)*          This means if E<7 GOTO line
(810+(E-6)*20))                                number 680+E*20 and if E>6
                                               GOTO line number
                                               (810+(E-6)*20).
```

ZX81 (Timex 1000) Conversation program

For the ZX81 you need a method of inputting all the data. You can do this with INPUT statements and loops. To run the program on the ZX81, make the following changes:

1. Make the same changes given for the Spectrum above, but put the DIM statements in lines 970-990.

2. Replace the READ/DATA lines with INPUT statements, e.g.

```
1000 REM PHRASES FOR PHRASE
CHECKING ROUTINE
1010 FOR I=1 TO 30
1020 INPUT Q$(I)
1030 NEXT I
```

3. Change line 1720 to read:

```
1720 STOP
```

4. Type the program in, then type RUN 970 and type in all the data as the computer asks you for it.

5. Then, to try the program, type GOTO 100. Do not press RUN, as if you do all the data will be lost.

6. Now you can save the program on cassette. When you load it, always type GOTO 100 to run the program.

Books about programming

The Usborne Guide to Better BASIC is a sequel to the Usborne Introduction to Computer Programming – a guide to the main BASIC commands for absolute beginners. Other books which you might find useful are:
Illustrating BASIC by Donald Alcock (Cambridge University Press, 1977)

Practise your BASIC by G. Waters and N. Cutler (Usborne, 1983)
Practical Things to do with a Microcomputer by J. Tatchell and N. Cutler (Usborne, 1983)
Brainteasers for BASIC computers by Gordon Lee (Shiva, 1983)

Answers

Robot runner puzzle (page 24)

```
10 INPUT "WHAT IS THE TEMPERATURE? ";TEMP
20 INPUT "HOW MANY SECONDS? ";S
30 IF TEMP<>60 THEN LET D=S*(500+10*(TEMP-60))
ELSE LET D=500*S
40 IF D<1 THEN PRINT "TOO COLD FOR ZAK"
50 PRINT "AT ";TEMP;" DEGREES, ZAK CAN
RUN ";D;" METRES IN ";S;" SECONDS"
```

The computer works out the 10*(TEMP−60) calculation first and this gives the difference in distance for TEMP degrees. (If TEMP is below 60, the answer to this calculation is negative.) Adding the answer to 500 gives the distance Zak can run in one second and multiplying by S gives distance in S seconds.

Shell sort swaps (page 34)

```
90 LET X=0
95 LET SWAP=0
231 LET X=X+1
271 LET SWAP=SWAP+1
365 PRINT "THERE WERE ";X;" COMPARISONS
AND ";SWAP;" EXCHANGES"
```

Wider bars (page 37)

```
285 FOR J=1 TO 8 STEP 2
290 PLOT INT(I*X+J),1
300 DRAW INT(I*X+J),INT(B(I)*Y)
310 PLOT INT(I*X-4-J),1
320 DRAW INT(I*X-4-J),INT(S(I)*Y)
325 NEXT J
```

You may need to change the figures to suit your computer.

Index

First published in 1983 by Usborne Publishing Ltd, 20 Garrick Street, London WC2E 9BJ.
© 1983 Usborne Publishing
The name Usborne and the device are Trade Marks of Usborne Publishing Ltd. All rights reserved. No part of this publication may be reproduced, stored in a retrieval system or transmitted in any form or by any means, electronic, mechanical, photocopying, recording or otherwise, without the prior permission of the publisher.
Printed in Spain by Printer Industria Gráfica, S.A.
Depósito Legal B-21527/1983